THE RINGS OF SATURN

W.G. Sebald was born in Wertach im Allgäu, in the Bavarian Alps, in 1944. He studied German language and literature in Freiburg, Switzerland and Manchester. In 1966 he took up a position as an assistant lecturer at the University of Manchester, settling permanently in England in 1970. He was professor of Modern German Literature at the University of East Anglia until his death in 2001.

Michael Hulse has translated Goethe's *The Sorrows of Young Werther* and Jacob Wasserman's *Caspar Hauser*, as well as the contemporary German authors Luise Rinser, Botho Strauss and Elfriede Jelinek. He is also an award-winning poet and, with John Kinsella, the editor of the literary magazine *Stand*. He lives in Amsterdam.

ALSO BY W.G. SEBALD

The Emigrants
Vertigo

W.G. Sebald

THE RINGS OF SATURN

Translated from the German by Michael Hulse

VINTAGE BOOKS

London

Published by Vintage 2002

10 9

First published with the title *Die Ringe des Saturn* by
Vito von Eichborn Verlag, Frankfurt am Main, 1995

First published in Great Britain in 1998 by
The Harvill Press

Vintage
Random House, 20 Vauxhall Bridge Road,
London SW1V 2SA

www.vintage-books.co.uk

Addresses for companies within The Random House Group Limited can be found at: www.randomhouse.co.uk/offices.htm

The Random House Group Limited Reg. No. 954009

A CIP catalogue record for this book
is available from the British Library

ISBN 9780099448921

The Random House Group Limited supports The Forest Stewardship Council (FSC), the leading international forest certification organisation. All our titles that are printed on Greenpeace approved FSC certified paper carry the FSC logo. Our paper procurement policy can be found at www.rbooks.co.uk/environment.

FSC
Mixed Sources
Product group from well-managed forests and other controlled sources
www.fsc.org Cert no. TT-COC-2139
© 1996 Forest Stewardship Council

Printed and bound in Great Britain by
CPI Bookmarque, Croydon, CR0 4TD

Il faut surtout pardonner à ces âmes malheureuses qui ont élu de faire le pèlerinage à pied, qui côtoient le rivage et regardent sans comprendre l'horreur de la lutte, la joie de vaincre ni le profond désespoir des vaincus.

JOSEPH CONRAD,
letter to Marguerite Poradowska,
23rd–25th March 1890

The rings of Saturn consist of ice crystals and probably meteorite particles describing circular orbits around the planet's equator. In all likelihood these are fragments of a former moon that was too close to the planet and was destroyed by its tidal effect (→ Roche limit).

Brockhaus Encyclopaedia

CONTENTS

I

In August 1992, when the dog days were drawing to an end, I set off to walk the county of Suffolk, in the hope of dispelling the emptiness that takes hold of me whenever I have completed a long stint of work. And in fact my hope was realized, up to a point; for I have seldom felt so carefree as I did then, walking for hours in the day through the thinly populated countryside, which stretches inland from the coast. I wonder now, however, whether there might be something in the old superstition that certain ailments of the spirit and of the body are particularly likely to beset us under the sign of the Dog Star. At all events, in retrospect I became preoccupied not only with the unaccustomed sense of freedom but also with the paralysing horror that had come over me at various times when confronted with the traces of destruction, reaching far back into the past, that were evident even in that remote place. Perhaps it was because of this that, a year to the day after I began my tour, I was taken into hospital in Norwich in a state of almost total immobility. It was then that I began in my thoughts to write these pages. I can remember precisely how, upon being admitted to that room on the eighth floor, I became overwhelmed by the feeling that the Suffolk expanses I had walked the previous summer had now shrunk once and for all to a single, blind, insensate spot. Indeed, all that could be seen of the world from my bed was the colourless patch of sky framed in the window.

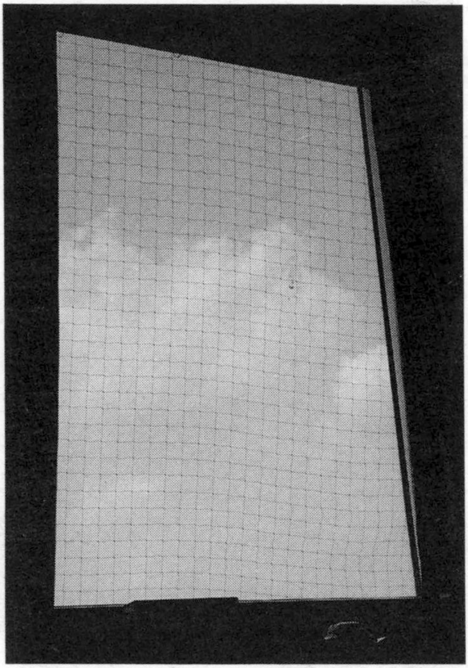

Several times during the day I felt a desire to assure myself of a reality I feared had vanished forever by looking out of that hospital window, which, for some strange reason, was draped with black netting, and as dusk fell the wish became so strong that, contriving to slip over the edge of the bed to the floor, half on my belly and half sideways, and then to reach the wall on all fours, I dragged myself, despite the pain, up to the window sill. In the tortured posture of a creature that has raised itself erect for the first time I stood leaning against the glass. I could not help thinking of the scene in which poor Gregor Samsa, his little legs trembling, climbs the armchair and looks out of his room, no longer remembering (so Kafka's narrative goes) the sense of liberation that gazing out of the window had formerly given him. And just as Gregor's dimmed eyes failed to recognize the quiet street where he and his family had lived for years, taking Charlottenstraße for a grey wasteland, so I too found the familiar city, extending from the hospital courtyards to the far horizon, an utterly alien place. I could not believe that anything might still be alive in that maze of buildings down there; rather, it was as if I were looking down from a cliff upon a sea of stone or a field of rubble, from which the tenebrous masses of multi-storey carparks rose up like immense boulders. At that twilit hour there were no passers-by to be seen in the immediate vicinity, but for a nurse crossing the cheerless gardens outside the hospital entrance on the way to her night shift. An ambulance with its light flashing was negotiating a number of turns on its way from the city centre to Casualty. I could not hear its siren; at that height I was cocooned in an almost complete and, as it were, artificial silence. All I could hear was the wind sweeping in from the country and buffeting the window; and in between, when the sound subsided, there was the never entirely ceasing murmur in my own ears.

Now that I begin to assemble my notes, more than a year after my discharge from hospital, I cannot help thinking of Michael

Parkinson who was, as I stood watching the city fade into the dying light, still alive in his small house in the Portersfield Road, busy perhaps, preparing a seminar or working on his study of Charles Ramuz, which had occupied him for many years. Michael was in his late forties, a bachelor, and, I believe, one of the most innocent people I have ever met. Nothing was ever further from his thoughts than self-interest; nothing troubled him quite so much as the dire responsibility of performing his duties, under increasingly adverse conditions. Above all, he was remarkable for the modesty of his needs, which some considered bordered on eccentricity. At a time when most people have constantly to be shopping in order to survive, Michael seemed to have no such need. Year in, year out, as long as I knew him, he wore either a navy blue or a rust-coloured jacket, and if the cuffs were frayed or the elbows threadbare he would sew on leather trims or patches. He even turned the collars of his shirts himself. In the summer vacations, Michael would make long walking tours of the Valais and the area around Lake Geneva, in connection with his Ramuz studies, and sometimes in the Jura or the Cévennes. It often seemed to me, when he returned from these travels or when I marvelled at the degree of dedication he always brought to his work, that in his own way he had found happiness, in a modest form that is scarcely conceivable nowadays. But then without warning last May Michael, who had not been seen for some days, was found dead in his bed, lying on his side and already quite rigid, his face curiously mottled with red blotches. The inquest concluded that he had died of unknown causes, a verdict to which I added the words, in the deep and dark hours of the night. The shock that went through us at this quite unexpected death affected no one more deeply than Janine Dakyns, who, like Michael, was a lecturer in Romance languages and unmarried too. Indeed, one might say that she was so unable to bear the loss of the ingenuous, almost childlike friendship they had shared, that a few weeks after his death she succumbed to a disease that swiftly consumed her body. Janine, who lived in a lane next to the hospital, had, like Michael, studied at Oxford and over the years had come to a profound understanding of the nineteenth-century French novel that had about it a certain private quality, wholly free of intellectual vanity and was guided by a fascination for obscure detail rather than by the self-evident. Gustave Flaubert was for her by far the finest of writers, and on many occasions she quoted long passages from the thousands of pages of his correspondence, never failing to astound me. Janine had taken an intense personal interest in the scruples which dogged Flaubert's writing, that fear of the false which, she said, sometimes kept him confined to his couch for weeks or months on end in the dread that he would never be able to write another word without compromising himself in the most grievous of ways. Moreover, Janine said, he was convinced that everything he had written hitherto consisted solely in a string of the most abysmal errors and lies, the consequences of which were immeasurable. Janine maintained that the source of Flaubert's scruples was to be found in the relentless spread of stupidity which he had observed everywhere, and which he believed had already invaded his own head. It was (so supposedly once he said) as if one was sinking into sand. This was probably the reason, she said, that sand possessed such significance in all of Flaubert's works. Sand conquered all. Time and again, said Janine, vast dust clouds drifted through Flaubert's dreams by day and by night, raised over the arid plains of the African continent and moving north across the Mediterranean and the Iberian peninsula till sooner or later they settled like ash from a fire on the Tuileries gardens, a suburb of Rouen or a country town in Normandy, penetrating into the tiniest crevices. In a grain of sand in the hem of Emma Bovary's winter gown, said Janine, Flaubert saw the whole of the Sahara. For him, every speck of dust weighed as heavy as the Atlas mountains. Many a time, at the end of a working day, Janine would talk to me about Flaubert's view of the world, in her office where there were such quantities of lecture notes, letters and other documents lying around that it was like standing amidst a flood of paper. On the desk, which was both the origin and the focal point of this amazing profusion of paper, a virtual paper landscape had come into being in the course of time, with mountains and valleys. Like a glacier when it reaches the sea, it had broken off at the edges and established new deposits all around on the floor, which in turn were advancing imperceptibly towards the centre of the room. Years ago, Janine had been obliged by the ever-increasing masses of paper on her desk to bring further tables into use, and these tables, where similar processes of accretion had subsequently taken place, represented later epochs, so to speak, in the evolution of Janine's paper universe. The carpet, too, had long since vanished beneath several inches of paper; indeed, the paper had begun climbing from the floor, on which, year after year, it had settled, and was now up the walls as high as the top of the door frame, page upon page of memoranda and notes pinned up in multiple layers, all of them by just one corner. Wherever it was possible there were piles of papers on the books on her shelves as well. It once occurred to me that at dusk, when all of this paper seemed to gather into itself the pallor of the fading light, it was like the snow in the fields, long ago, beneath the ink-black sky. In the end Janine was reduced to working from an easychair drawn more or less into the middle of her room where, if one passed her door, which was always ajar, she could be seen bent almost double scribbling on a pad on her knees or sometimes just lost in thought. Once when I remarked that sitting there amidst her papers she resembled the angel in Dürer's *Melancholia*, steadfast among the instruments of destruction, her response was that the apparent chaos surrounding her represented in reality a perfect kind of order, or an order which at least tended towards perfection. And the fact was that whatever she might be looking for amongst her papers or her books, or in her head, she was generally able to find right away. It was Janine who referred me to the surgeon Anthony Batty Shaw, whom she knew from the Oxford Society, when after my discharge from hospital I began my enquiries about Thomas Browne, who had practised as a doctor in Norwich in the seventeenth century and had left a number of writings that defy all comparison. An entry in the 1911 edition of the *Encyclopaedia Britannica* had told me that Browne's skull was kept in the museum of the Norfolk & Norwich Hospital. Unequivocal though this claim appeared, my attempts to locate the skull in the very place where until recently I had been a patient met with no success, for none of the ladies and gentlemen of the present administrative staff at the hospital was aware that any such museum existed. Not only did they stare at me in utter incomprehension when I voiced my strange request, but I even had the impression that some of those I asked thought of me as an eccentric crank. Yet it is well known that in the period when public health and hygiene were being reformed and hospitals established, many of these institutions kept museums, or rather chambers of horrors, in which prematurely born, deformed or hydrocephalic foetuses, hypertrophied organs, and other items of a similar nature were preserved in jars of formaldehyde, for medical purposes, and occasionally exhibited to the public. The question was where the things had got to. The local history section of the main library, which has since been destroyed by fire, was unable to give me any information concerning the Norfolk & Norwich Hospital and the whereabouts of Browne's skull. It was not until I made contact with Anthony Batty Shaw, through Janine, that I obtained the information I was after. Thomas Browne, so Batty Shaw wrote in an article he sent me which he had just published in the *Journal of Medical Biography*, died in 1682 on his seventy-seventh birthday and was buried in the parish church of St Peter Mancroft in Norwich. There his mortal remains lay undisturbed until 1840, when the coffin was damaged during preparations for another burial in the chancel, and its contents partially exposed. As a result, Browne's skull and a lock of his hair passed into the possession of one Dr Lubbock, a parish councillor, who in turn left the relics in his will to the hospital museum, where they were put on display amidst various anatomical curiosities until 1921 under a bell jar. It was not until then that St Peter Mancroft's repeated request for the return of Browne's skull was acceded to, and, almost a quarter of a millennium after the first burial, a second interment was performed with all due ceremony. Curiously enough, Browne himself, in his famous part-archaeological and part-metaphysical treatise, *Urn Burial*, offers the most fitting commentary on the subsequent odyssey of his own skull when he writes that to be gnaw'd out of our graves is a tragical abomination. But, he adds, who is to know the fate of his bones, or how often he is to be buried?

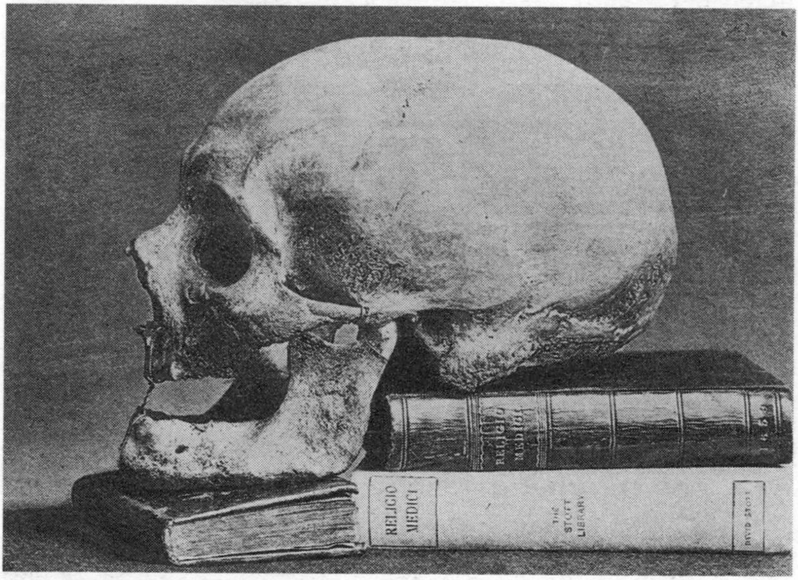

Thomas Browne was born in London on the 19th of October 1605, the son of a silk merchant. Little is known of his childhood, and the accounts of his life following completion of his master's degree at Oxford tell us scarcely anything about the nature of his later medical studies. All we know for certain is that from his twenty-fifth to his twenty-eighth year he attended the universities of Montpellier, Padua and Vienna, then outstanding in the Hippocratic sciences, and that just before returning to England, received a doctorate in medicine from Leiden. In January 1632, while Browne was in Holland, and thus at a time when he was engaging more profoundly with the mysteries of the human body than ever before, the dissection of a corpse was undertaken in public at the Waaggebouw in Amsterdam – the body being that of Adriaan Adriaanszoon alias Aris Kindt, a petty thief of that city who had been hanged for his misdemeanours an hour or so earlier. Although we have no definite evidence for this, it is probable that Browne would have heard of the dissection and was present at the extraordinary event, which Rembrandt depicted in his painting of the Guild of Surgeons, for the anatomy lessons given every year in the depth of winter by Dr Nicolaas Tulp were not only of the greatest interest to a student of medicine but constituted in addition a significant date in the agenda of a society that saw itself as emerging from the darkness into the light. The spectacle, presented before a paying public drawn from the upper classes, was no doubt a demonstration of the undaunted investigative zeal in the new sciences; but it also represented (though this surely would have been refuted) the archaic ritual of dismembering a corpse, of harrowing the flesh of the delinquent even beyond death, a procedure then still part of the ordained punishment.

That the anatomy lesson in Amsterdam was about more than a thorough knowledge of the inner organs of the human body is suggested by Rembrandt's representation of the ceremonial nature of the dissection – the surgeons are in their finest attire, and Dr Tulp is wearing a hat on his head – as well as by the fact that afterwards there was a formal, and in a sense symbolic, banquet. If we stand today before the large canvas of Rembrandt's *The Anatomy Lesson* in the Mauritshuis we are standing precisely where those who were present at the dissection in the Waaggebouw stood, and we believe that we see what they saw then: in the foreground, the greenish, prone body of Aris Kindt, his neck broken and his chest risen terribly in rigor mortis. And yet it is debatable whether anyone ever really saw that body, since the art of anatomy, then in its infancy, was not least a way of making the reprobate body invisible. It is somehow odd that Dr Tulp's colleagues are not looking at Kindt's body, that their gaze is directed just past it to focus on the open anatomical atlas in which the appalling physical facts are reduced to a diagram, a schematic plan of the human being, such as envisaged by the enthusiastic amateur anatomist René Descartes, who was also, so it is said, present that January morning in the Waaggebouw. In his philosophical investigations, which form one of the principal chapters of the history of subjection, Descartes teaches that one should disregard the flesh, which is beyond our comprehension, and attend to the machine within, to what can fully be understood, be made wholly useful for work, and, in the event of any fault, either repaired or discarded.

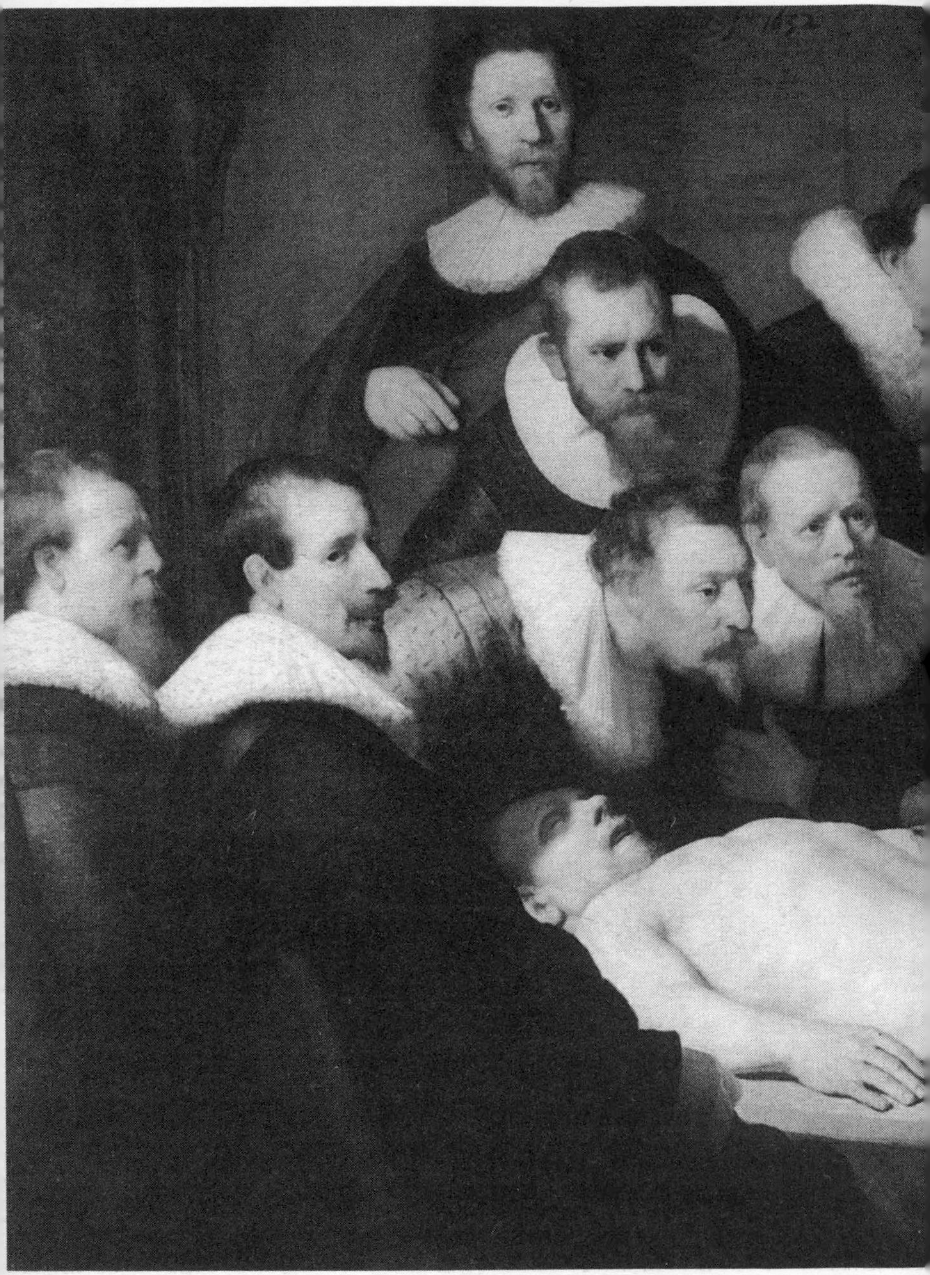

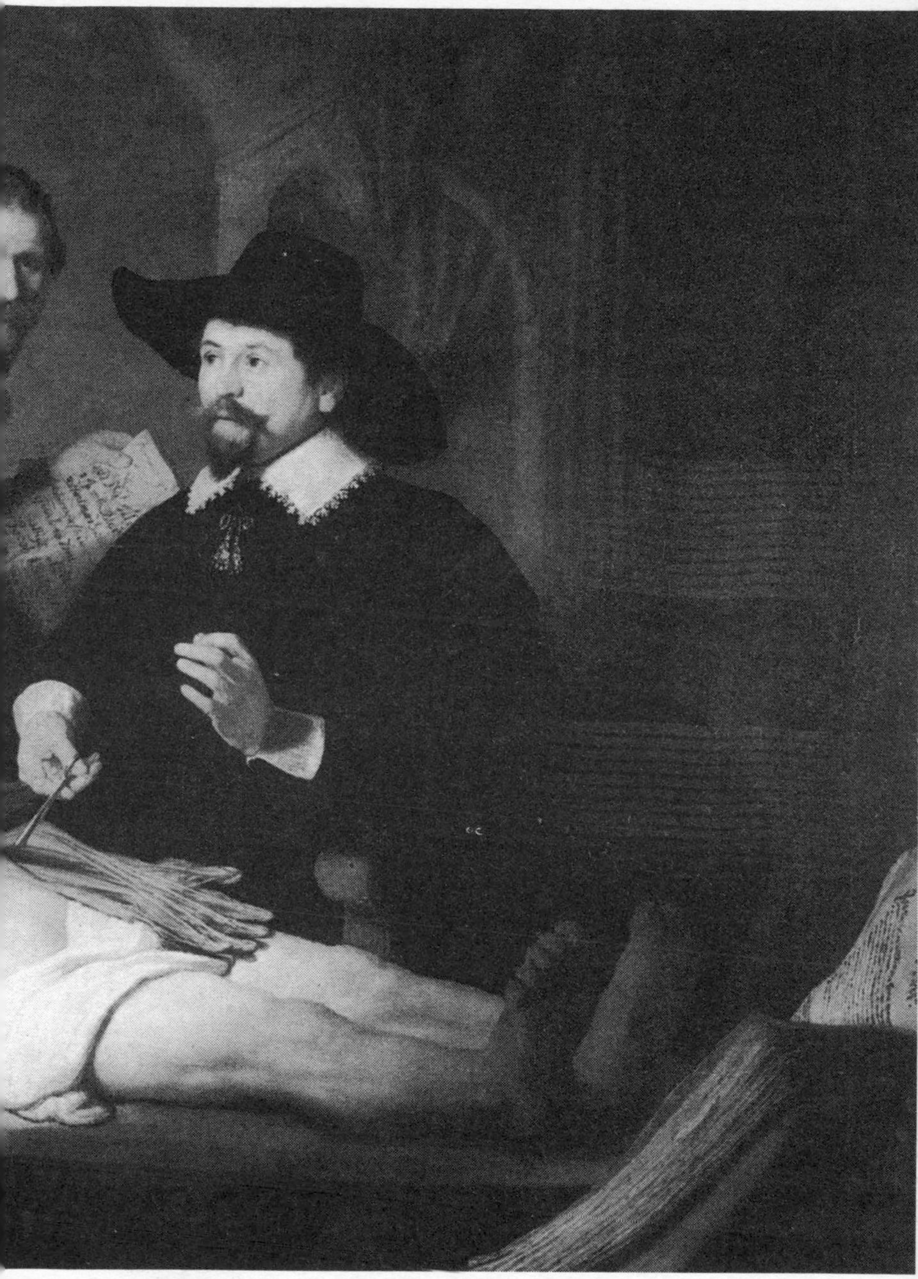

Though the body is open to contemplation, it is, in a sense, excluded, and in the same way the much-admired verisimilitude of Rembrandt's picture proves on closer examination to be more apparent than real. Contrary to normal practice, the anatomist shown here has not begun his dissection by opening the abdomen and removing the intestines, which are most prone to putrefaction, but has started (and this too may imply a punitive dimension to the act) by dissecting the offending hand. Now, this hand is most peculiar. It is not only grotesquely out of proportion compared with

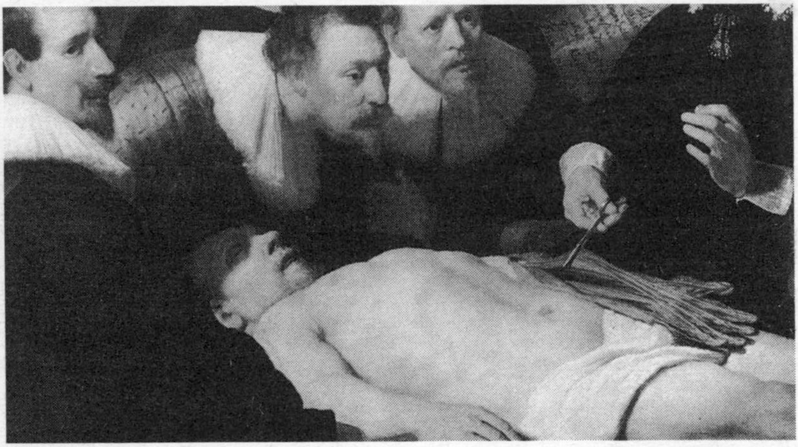

the hand closer to us, but it is also anatomically the wrong way round: the exposed tendons, which ought to be those of the left palm, given the position of the thumb, are in fact those of the back of the right hand. In other words, what we are faced with is a transposition taken from the anatomical atlas, evidently without further reflection, that turns this otherwise true-to-life painting (if one may so express it) into a crass misrepresentation at the exact centre point of its meaning, where the incisions are made. It seems inconceivable that we are faced here with an unfortunate blunder. Rather, I believe that there was deliberate intent behind this flaw in the composition. That unshapely hand signifies the violence that has been done to Aris Kindt. It is with him, the victim, and not the Guild that gave Rembrandt his commission, that the painter identifies. His gaze alone is free of Cartesian rigidity. He alone sees that greenish annihilated body, and he alone sees the shadow in the half-open mouth and over the dead man's eyes.

We have no evidence to tell us from which angle Thomas Browne watched the dissection, if, as I believe, he was among the onlookers in the anatomy theatre in Amsterdam, or indeed what he might have seen there. Perhaps, as Browne says in a later note about the great fog that shrouded large parts of England and Holland on the 27th of November 1674, it was the white mist that rises from within a body opened presently after death, and which during our lifetime, so he adds, clouds our brain when asleep and dreaming. I still recall how my own consciousness was veiled by the same sort of fog as I lay in my hospital room once more after surgery late in the evening. Under the wonderful influence of the painkillers coursing through me, I felt, in my iron-framed bed, like a balloonist floating weightless amidst the mountainous clouds towering on every side. At times the billowing masses would part and I gazed out at the indigo vastness and down into the depths where I supposed the earth to be, a black and impenetrable maze. But in the firmament above were the stars, tiny points of gold speckling the barren wastes. Through the resounding emptiness, my ears caught the voices of the two nurses who took my pulse and from time to time moistened my lips with a small, pink sponge attached to a stick, which reminded me of the Turkish Delight lollipops we used to buy at the fair. Katy and Lizzie were the names of these ministering angels, and I think I have rarely been as elated as I was in their care that night. Of the everyday matters they chatted about I understood very little. All I heard was the rise and fall of their voices, a kind of warbling such as comes from the throats of birds, a perfect, fluting sound, part celestial and part the song of sirens. Of all the things Katy said to Lizzie and Lizzie to Katy, I remember only one odd scrap. I think Katy, or Lizzie, was describing a holiday on Malta where, she said, the Maltese, with a death-defying insouciance quite beyond comprehension, drove neither on the left nor on the right, but always on the shady side of the road. It was not until dawn, when the morning shift relieved the night nurses, that I realized where I was. I became aware again of my body, the insensate foot, and the pain in my back; I heard the rattle of crockery as the hospital's daily routine started in the corridor; and, as the first light brightened the sky, I saw a vapour trail cross the segment framed by my window. At the time I took that white trail for a good omen, but now, as I look back, I fear it marked the beginning of a fissure that has since riven my life. The aircraft at the tip of the trail was as invisible as the passengers inside it. The invisibility and intangibility of that which moves us remained an unfathomable mystery for Thomas Browne too, who saw our world as no more than a shadow image of another one far beyond. In his thinking and writing he therefore sought to look upon earthly existence, from the things that were closest to him to the spheres of the universe, with the eye of an outsider, one might even say of the creator. His only means of achieving the sublime heights that this endeavour required was a parlous loftiness in his language. In common with other English writers of the seventeenth century, Browne wrote out of the fullness of his erudition, deploying a vast repertoire of quotations and the names of authorities who had gone before, creating complex metaphors and analogies, and constructing labyrinthine sentences that sometimes extend over one or two pages, sentences that resemble processions or a funeral cortège in their sheer ceremonial lavishness. It is true that, because of the immense weight of the impediments he is carrying, Browne's writing can be held back by the force of gravitation, but when he does succeed in rising higher and higher through the circles of his spiralling prose, borne aloft like a glider on warm currents of air, even today the reader is overcome by a sense of levitation. The greater the distance, the clearer the view: one sees the tiniest of details with the utmost clarity. It is as if one were looking through a reversed opera glass and through a microscope at the same time. And yet, says Browne, all knowledge is enveloped in darkness. What we perceive are no more than isolated lights in the abyss of ignorance, in the shadow-filled edifice of the world. We study the order of things, says Browne, but we cannot grasp their innermost essence. And because it is so, it befits our philosophy to be writ small, using the shorthand and contracted forms of transient Nature, which alone are a reflection of eternity. True to his own prescription, Browne records the patterns which recur in the seemingly infinite diversity of forms; in *The Garden of Cyrus,* for instance, he draws the quincunx,

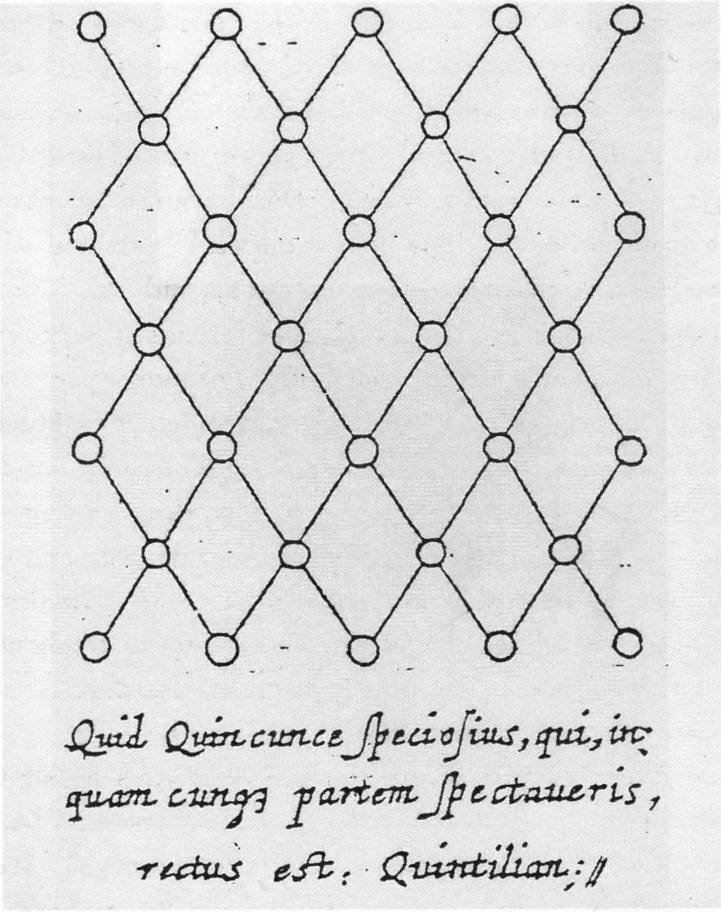
Quid Quincunce speciosius, qui, in
quam cunq; partem spectaueris,
rectus est: Quintilian:

which is composed by using the corners of a regular quadrilateral and the point at which its diagonals intersect. Browne identifies this structure everywhere, in animate and inanimate matter: in certain crystalline forms, in starfish and sea urchins, in the vertebrae of mammals and the backbones of birds and fish, in the skins of various species of snake, in the crosswise prints left by quadrupeds, in the physical shapes of caterpillars, butterflies, silkworms and moths, in the root of the water fern, in the seed husks of the sunflower and the Caledonian pine, within young oak shoots or the stem of the horsetail; and in the creations of mankind, in the pyramids of Egypt and the mausoleum of Augustus as in the garden of King Solomon, which was planted with mathematical precision with pomegranate trees and white lilies. Examples might be multiplied without end, says Browne, and one might demonstrate *ad infinitum* the elegant geometrical designs of Nature; however – thus, with a fine turn of phrase and image, he concludes his treatise – the constellation of the Hyades, the Quincunx of Heaven, is already sinking beneath the horizon, and so 'tis time to close the five ports of knowledge. We are unwilling to spin out our waking thoughts into the phantasmes of sleep; making cables of cobwebs and wildernesses of handsome groves. Besides, he adds, Hippocrates in his notes on sleeplessness has spoken so little of the miracle of plants, that there is scant encouragement to dream of Paradise, not least since in practice we are occupied above all by the abnormalities of creation, be they the deformities produced by sickness or the grotesqueries with which Nature, with an inventiveness scarcely less diseased, fills every vacant space in her atlas. And indeed, while on the one hand the study of Nature today aims to describe a system governed by immutable laws, on the other it delights in drawing our attention to creatures noteworthy for their bizarre physical form or behaviour. Even in Brehm's *Thierleben*, a popular nineteenth-century zoological compendium, pride of place is given to the crocodile and the kangaroo, the ant-eater and the armadillo, the seahorse and the pelican; and nowadays we are shown on the television screen a colony of penguins, say, standing motionless through the long dark winter of the Antarctic, with its icy storms, on their feet the eggs laid at a milder time of year. In programmes of this kind, which are called *Nature Watch* or *Survival* and are considered particularly educational, one is more likely to see some monster coupling at the bottom of Lake Baikal than an ordinary blackbird. Thomas Browne too was often distracted from his investigations into the isomorphic line of the quincunx by singular phenomena that fired his curiosity, and by work on a comprehensive pathology. He is said to have long kept a bittern in his study in order to find out how this peculiar bird could produce from the depths of its throat such a strange bassoon-like sound, unique in the whole of Nature; and in the *Pseudodoxia Epidemica*, in which he dispels popular errors and legends, he deals with beings both real and imaginary, such as the chameleon, the salamander, the ostrich, the gryphon and the phoenix, the basilisk, the unicorn, and the amphisbaena, the serpent with two heads. In most cases, Browne refutes the existence of the fabled creatures, but the astonishing monsters that we know to be properly part of the natural world leave us with a suspicion that even the most fantastical beasts might not be mere inventions. At all events, it is clear from Browne's account that the endless mutations of Nature, which go far beyond any rational limit, and equally the chimaeras produced by our own minds, were as much a source of fascination to him as they were, three-hundred years later, to Jorge Luis Borges, whose *Libro de los seres imaginarios* was published in Buenos Aires in 1967. Recently I realized that the imaginary beings listed alphabetically in that compendium include the creature

Baldanders, whom Simplicius Simplicissimus encounters in the sixth book of Grimmelshausen's narrative. There, Baldanders is first seen as a stone sculpture lying in a forest, resembling a Germanic hero of old and wearing a Roman soldier's tunic with a big Swabian bib. Baldanders claims to have come from Paradise, to have always been in Simplicius's company, unbeknownst to him, and to be unable to quit his side until Simplicius shall have reverted to the clay he is made of. Then, before the very eyes of Simplicius, Baldanders changes into a scribe who writes these lines,

Ich bin der Anfang und das End
und gelte
an allen Ortyen.

Manoha · gilos, timad, iſaſer, ſale, lacob, ſalet,
enni nacob idil dadele neuaco ide eges Eli neme
meodi eledid emonatan deſi negogag editor goga
naneg eriden, hohe ritatan auilac, hohe ilamen e-
riden diledi liſac uſur ſodaled auar, amu ſaliſono-
nor macheli retoran; Vlidon dad amu oſſoſſon,
Gedal amu bede neuavv, alijs, dilede ronodavv
agnoh tegnoh eni tatæ hyn lamini celotah, iſis to-
loſtabas oronatah aſſis tobulu, VViera ſaladid egri-
vi nanon ægar rimini ſiſac, helioſole Ramelu o-
nonor vvindelishi timinitur, bagoge gagoe hane-
nor elimitat.

and then into a mighty oak, a sow, a sausage, a piece of excrement, a field of clover, a white flower, a mulberry tree, and a silk carpet. Much as in this continuous process of consuming and being consumed, nothing endures, in Thomas Browne's view. On every new thing there lies already the shadow of annihilation. For the history of every individual, of every social order, indeed of the whole world, does not describe an ever-widening, more and more wonderful arc, but rather follows a course which, once the meridian is reached, leads without fail down into the dark. Knowledge of that descent into the dark, for Browne, is inseparable from his belief in the day of resurrection, when, as in a theatre, the last revolutions are ended and the actors appear once more on stage, to complete and make up the catastrophe of this great piece. As a doctor, who saw disease growing and raging in bodies, he understood mortality better than the flowering of life. To him it seems a miracle that we should last so much as a single day. There is no antidote, he writes, against the opium of time. The winter sun shows how soon the light fades from the ash, how soon night enfolds us. Hour upon hour is added to the sum. Time itself grows old. Pyramids, arches and obelisks are melting pillars of snow. Not even those who have found a place amidst the heavenly constellations have perpetuated their names: Nimrod is lost in Orion, and Osiris in the Dog Star. Indeed, old families last not three oaks. To set one's name to a work gives no one a title to be remembered, for who knows how many of the best of men have gone without a trace? The iniquity of oblivion blindly scatters her poppyseed and when wretchedness falls upon us one summer's day like snow, all we wish for is to be forgotten. These are the circles Browne's thoughts describe, most unremittingly perhaps in the *Hydriotaphia* or *Urn Burial* of 1658, a discourse on sepulchral urns found in a field near Walsingham in Norfolk. Drawing upon the most varied of historical and natural historical sources, he expatiates upon the rites we enact when one from our midst sets out on his last journey. Beginning with some examples of sepulture in elephants, cranes, the sepulchral cells of pismires and practice of bees; which civil society carrieth out their dead, and hath exequies, if not interments, he describes the funeral rites of numerous peoples before coming to the Christian religion, which buries the sinful body whole and thus extinguishes the fires once and for all. The almost universal practice of cremation in pre-Christian times should not lead one to conclude, as is often done, that the heathen were ignorant of life beyond death, to show which Browne observes that the funeral pyres were built of sweet fuel, cypress, fir, yew, and other trees perpetually verdant as silent expressions of their surviving hopes. Browne also remarks that, contrary to general belief, it is not difficult to burn a human body: a piece of an old boat burnt Pompey, and the King of Castile burnt large numbers of Saracens with next to no fuel, the fire being visible far and wide. Indeed, he adds, if the burthen of Isaac were sufficient for an holocaust, a man may carry his own pyre. Browne then turns to the strange vessels unearthed from the field near Walsingham. It is astounding, he says, how long these thin-walled clay urns remained intact a yard underground, while the sword and ploughshare passed above them and great buildings, palaces and cloud-high towers crumbled and collapsed. The cremated remains in the urns are examined closely: the ash, the loose teeth, some long roots of quitch, or dog's grass wreathed about the bones, and the coin intended for the Elysian ferryman. Browne records other objects known to have been placed with the dead, whether as ornament or utensil. His catalogue includes a variety of curiosities: the circumcision knives of Joshua, the ring which belonged to the mistress of Propertius, an ape of agate, a grasshopper, three-hundred golden bees, a blue opal, silver belt buckles and clasps, combs, iron pins, brass plates and brazen nippers to pull away hair, and a brass jew's-harp that last sounded on the crossing over the black water. The most marvellous item, however, from a Roman urn preserved by Cardinal Farnese, is a drinking glass, so bright it might have been newly blown. For Browne, things of this kind, unspoiled by the passage of time, are symbols of the indestructibility of the human soul assured by scripture, which the physician, firm though he may be in his Christian faith, perhaps secretly doubts. And since the heaviest stone that melancholy can throw at a man is to tell him he is at the end of his nature, Browne scrutinizes that which escaped annihilation for any sign of the mysterious capacity for transmigration he has so often observed in caterpillars and moths. That purple piece of silk he refers to, then, in the urn of Patroclus – what does it mean?

II

It was on a grey, overcast day in August 1992 that I travelled down to the coast in one of the old diesel trains, grimed with oil and soot up to the windows, which ran from Norwich to Lowestoft at that time. The few passengers that there were sat in the half-light on the threadbare seats, all of them facing the engine and as far away from each other as they could be, and so silent, that not a word might have passed their lips in the whole of their lives. Most of the time the carriage, pitching about unsteadily on the track, was merely coasting along, since there is an almost unbroken gentle decline towards the sea; at intervals, though, when the gears engaged with a jolt that rocked the entire framework, the grinding of cog wheels could be heard for a while, till, with a more even pounding, the onward roll resumed, past the back gardens, allotments, rubbish dumps and factory yards to the east of the city and out into the marshes beyond. Through Brundall, Buckenham and Cantley, where, at the end of a straight roadway, a sugar-beet refinery with a belching smokestack sits in a green field like a steamer at a wharf, the line follows the River

Yare, till at Reedham it crosses the water and, in a wide curve, enters the vast flatland that stretches southeast down to the sea. Save for the odd solitary cottage there is nothing to be seen but the grass and the rippling reeds, one or two sunken willows, and some ruined conical brick buildings, like relics of an extinct civilization. These are all that remains of the countless wind pumps and windmills whose white sails revolved over the marshes of

Halvergate and all along the coast until in the decades following the First World War, one after the other, they were all shut down. It's hard to imagine now, I was once told by someone who could remember the turning sails in his childhood, that the white flecks of the windmills lit up the landscape just as a tiny highlight brings life to a painted eye. And when those bright little points faded away, the whole region, so to speak, faded with them. – After Reedham we stopped at Haddiscoe and

Herringfleet, two scattered villages just visible in the distance; and at the next station, the halt for Somerleyton Hall, I got out. The train ground into motion again and disappeared round a gradual bend, leaving a trail of black smoke behind it. There was no station at the stop, only an open shelter. I walked down the deserted platform, to my left the seemingly endless expanses of the marshes and to my right, beyond a low brick wall, the shrubs and trees of the park. There was not a soul about, of whom one might have asked the way. At one time, I thought, as I slung my rucksack over my shoulder and crossed the track, things would have been quite different here. Almost everything a residence such as Somerleyton required for its proper upkeep and all that was necessary in order to sustain a social position never altogether secure would have been brought in on the railway from other parts of the country and would have arrived at this station in the goods van of the olive-green-liveried steam train – furnishings, equipment and impedimenta of every description, the new piano, curtains and portières, the Italian tiles and fittings for the bathrooms, the boiler and pipes for the hothouses, supplies from the market gardens, cases of hock and Bordeaux, lawn mowers and great boxes of whalebone corsets and crinolines from London. And now there was nothing any more, nobody, no stationmaster in gleaming peaked cap, no servants, no coachman, no house guests, no shooting parties, neither gentlemen in indestructible tweeds nor ladies in stylish travelling clothes. It takes just one awful second, I often think, and an entire epoch passes. Nowadays Somerleyton Hall, like most important country houses, is open to a paying public in the summer months. But these people do not arrive by the diesel train; they drive in at the main gates in their own automobiles. If one nevertheless arrives at the railway halt, as I did, and has no desire to walk all the way round to the front, one has to climb the wall like some interloper and struggle through the thicket before reaching the park. It seemed to me like a curious object lesson from the history of evolution, which at times repeats its earlier conceits with a certain sense of irony, that when I emerged from the trees I beheld a miniature train puffing through the fields with a number of people sitting on it. They reminded me of dressed-up circus dogs or seals; and at the front of the train, a ticket satchel slung about him, sat the engine driver, conductor and controller of all the animals, the present Lord Somerleyton, Her Majesty The Queen's Master of the Horse.

In the Middle Ages, the manor of Somerleyton was held by the FitzOsberts and the Jernegans, but over the centuries ownership of the estate passed to a number of families related either by blood or by marriage. From the Jernegans it fell to the Wentworths, from the Wentworths to the Garneys, from the Garneys to the Allens, and from the Allens to the Anguishes, whose line became extinct in 1843. In that year, Lord Sydney Godolphin Osborne, a distant relative of that extinct family, chose not to take up his inheritance and instead sold the entire property to Sir Morton Peto. Peto, who came of humble origins and who had worked his way up from bricklayer's labourer, was just thirty when he purchased Somerleyton, but was already among the foremost entrepreneurs and speculators of his time. In the planning and execution of prestigious construction projects in London, among them Hungerford Market, the Reform Club, Nelson's Column and a number of West End theatres, he set new standards in every respect. Moreover, his financial interests in the railways being built in Canada, Australia, Africa, Argentina, Russia and Norway had made him a truly massive fortune in the shortest of times, so that he was now ready to crown his ascent into the highest social spheres by establishing a country residence, the comfort and extravagance of which would eclipse everything the nation had hitherto seen. And indeed Morton Peto's dream, a princely palace in what was known as the Anglo-Italian style, along with its interiors, was completed within a very few years on the site of the old, demolished hall. As early as 1852, *The Illustrated London News* and other society periodicals were running the most effusive reports on the new Somerleyton. In particular, it was famed for the scarcely perceptible transitions from interiors to exterior; those who visited were barely able to tell where the natural ended and the man-made began. There were drawing rooms and winter gardens, spacious halls and verandahs. A corridor might end in a ferny grotto where fountains ceaselessly plashed, and bowered passages criss-crossed beneath the dome of a fantastic mosque. Windows could be lowered to open the interior onto the outside, and inside the landscape was replicated on the mirror walls. Palm houses and orangeries, the lawn like green velvet, the baize on the billiard tables, the bouquets of flowers in the morning and retiring rooms and in the majolica vases on the terrace, the birds of paradise and the golden pheasants on the silken tapestries, the goldfinches in the aviaries and the nightingales in the garden, the arabesques in the carpets and the box-edged flower beds – all of it interacted in such a way that one had the illusion of complete harmony between the natural and the manufactured. The most wonderful sight of all, according to one contemporary description, was Somerleyton of a summer's night, when the incomparable glasshouses, borne on cast-iron pillars and braces and seemingly weightless in their filigree grace, shed their gleaming radiance on the dark. Countless Argand burners backed with silver-plated reflectors, the white flames consuming the poisonous gas with a low hissing sound, cast an immense brightness that pulsated like the current of life that runs through the earth.

Not even Coleridge, in an opium dream, could have imagined a more magical scene for his Mongol overlord, Kubla Khan. And now, the writer continues, suppose that at some point during a soirée you and someone close to you climb the campanile at Somerleyton, you stand on the gallery at the very top and are brushed by the soundless wing of a bird gliding by in the night!

The intoxicating scent of linden blossom is wafted up from the great avenue. Below, you see the steep roofs tiled with dark blue slate, and in the snow-white glow from the shimmering glasshouses the level blackness of the lawns. Further off in the park drift the shadows of Lebanese cedars; in the deer enclosure, the wary animals keep one eye open in their sleep; and beyond the furthermost perimeter, away toward the horizon, the marshes extend and the sails of the mills are turning in the wind.

Somerleyton strikes the visitor of today no longer as an oriental palace in a fairy tale. The glass-covered walks and the palm house, whose lofty dome used once to light up the nights, were burnt out in 1913 after a gas explosion and subsequently demolished. The servants who kept all in good order, the butlers, coachmen, chauffeurs, gardeners, cooks, sempstresses and chambermaids, have long since gone. The suites of rooms now make a somewhat disused, dispirited impression. The velvet curtains and crimson blinds are faded, the settees and armchairs sag, the stairways and corridors which the guided tour takes one through are full of bygone paraphernalia. A camphorwood chest which may once have accompanied a former occupant of the house on a tour of duty to Nigeria or Singapore now contains old croquet mallets and wooden balls, golf clubs, billiard cues and tennis racquets, most of them so small they might have been intended for children, or have shrunk in the course of the years. The walls are hung with copper kettles, bedpans, hussars' sabres, African masks, spears, safari trophies, hand-coloured engravings of Boer War battles – *Battle of Pieters Hill and Relief of Ladysmith: A Bird's-Eye View from an Observation Balloon* – and a number of family portraits painted perhaps some time between 1920 and 1960 by an artist not untouched by Modernism, the plaster-coloured faces of the sitters mottled with scarlet and purple blotches. The stuffed polar bear in the entrance hall stands over three yards tall. With its yellowish and moth-eaten fur, it resembles a ghost bowed by sorrows. There are indeed moments, as one passes through the rooms open to the public at Somerleyton, when one is not quite sure whether one is in a country house in Suffolk or some kind of no-man's-land, on the shores of the Arctic Ocean or in the heart of the dark continent. Nor can one readily say which decade or century it is, for many ages are superimposed here and coexist. As I strolled through Somerleyton Hall that August afternoon, amidst a throng of visitors who occasionally lingered here or there, I was variously reminded of a pawnbroker's or an auction hall. And yet it was the sheer number of things, possessions accumulated by generations and now waiting, as it were, for the day when they would be sold off, that won me over to what was, ultimately, a collection of oddities. How uninviting Somerleyton must have been, I reflected, in the days of the industrial impresario Morton Peto, MP, when everything, from the cellar to the attic, from the cutlery to the waterclosets, was brand new, matching in every detail, and in unremittingly good taste. And how fine a place the house seemed to me now that it was imperceptibly nearing the brink of dissolution and silent oblivion. However, on emerging into the open air again, I was saddened to see, in one of the otherwise deserted aviaries, a solitary Chinese quail, evidently in a state of dementia, running to and fro along the edge of the cage and shaking its head every time it was about to turn, as if it could not comprehend how it had got into this hopeless fix.

The grounds, in contrast to the waning splendour of the house, were now at their evolutionary peak, a century after the heyday of Somerleyton. The flower beds might well have been better tended and more gloriously colourful, but today the trees planted by Morton Peto filled the air above the gardens, and several of the ancient cedars, which were there to be admired by visitors even then, now extended their branches over well-nigh a quarter of an acre, each an entire world unto itself. There were sequoias towering more than sixty yards, and rare oriental planes, the outermost extremities of which had bowed down as low as the lawn, securing a hold where they touched the ground, to shoot up once more in a perfect circle. It was easy to imagine this species of plane tree spreading over the country, just as concentric circles ripple across water, the parents becoming weaker and dying off from within as the progeny conquers the land about them. Some of the lighter-coloured trees seemed to drift like clouds above the parkland. Others were of a deep, impenetrable green. Like terraces the crowns rose one upon another, and if one defocused one's eyes just slightly it was like looking upon mountains covered with vast forests. Yet the densest and greenest was for me the Somerleyton yew maze, in the heart of the mysterious estate, where I became so completely lost that I could not find the way out again until I resorted to drawing a line with the heel of my boot across the white sand of every hedged passage that had proved to be a dead end. Later, in one of the long hothouses built against the brick walls of the kitchen garden, I struck up a conversation with William Hazel, the gardener who now looks after Somerleyton with the help of several odd-jobmen. When he realized where I was from he told me that during his last years at school, and his subsequent apprenticeship, his thoughts constantly revolved around the bombing raids then being launched on Germany from the sixty-seven airfields that were established in East Anglia after 1940. People nowadays hardly have any idea of the scale of the operation, said Hazel. In the course of one thousand and nine days, the eighth airfleet alone used a billion gallons of fuel, dropped seven hundred and thirty-two thousand tons of bombs, and lost almost nine thousand aircraft and fifty thousand men. Every evening I watched the bomber squadrons heading out over Somerleyton, and night after night, before I went to sleep, I pictured in my mind's eye the German cities going up in flames, the firestorms setting the heavens alight, and the survivors rooting about in the ruins. One day when Lord Somerleyton was helping me prune the vines in this green-house, for something to do, said Hazel, he explained the Allied carpet-bombing strategy to me, and some time later he brought me a big relief map of Germany. All the place names I had heard on the news were marked in strange letters alongside symbolic pictures of the towns that varied in the number of gables, turrets and towers according to the size of the population; and moreover, in the case of particularly important cities, there were emblems of features associated with them, such as Cologne cathedral, the Römer in Frankfurt, or the statue of Roland in Bremen. Those tiny images of towns, about the size of postage stamps, looked like romantic castles, and I pictured the German Reich as a medieval and vastly enigmatic land. Time and again I studied the various regions on the map, from the Polish border to the Rhine, from the green plains of the north to the dark brown Alps, partly covered with eternal snow and ice, and spelled out the names of the cities, the destruction of which had just been announced: Braunschweig and Würzburg, Wilhelmshaven, Schweinfurt, Stuttgart, Pforzheim, Düren, and dozens more. In that way I got to know the whole country by heart; you might even say it was burnt into me. At all events, ever since then I have tried to find out everything I could that was in any way connected with the war in the air. In the early Fifties, when I was in Lüneburg with the army of occupation, I even learnt German, after a fashion, so that I could read what the Germans themselves had said about the bombings and their lives in the ruined cities. To my astonishment, however, I soon found the search for such accounts invariably proved fruitless. No one at the time seemed to have written about their experiences or afterwards recorded their memories. Even if you asked people directly, it was as if everything had been erased from their minds. As for myself, though, whenever I close my eyes, to this day, I see the formations of bombers, Lancasters and Halifaxes, Liberators and Flying Fortresses, going out towards Germany across the grey North Sea, and then straggling home in the dawn. In early April 1945, not long before the War ended, said Hazel, sweeping up the vine shoots he had cut, I saw two American Thunderbolts crash here, over Somerleyton. It was a fine Sunday morning. I had been helping my father with an urgent repair job up on the campanile, which is really a water tower. When we were finished we stood on the look-out platform, from where there is a view right out to sea. We had hardly had time to look around when the two planes, returning from a patrol, staged a dogfight over the estate, out of sheer high spirits, I suppose. We could see the pilots' faces clearly in their cockpits. The engines roared as they chased after each other, or flew side by side in the bright spring air, till their wing tips touched as they banked. It had seemed like a friendly game, said Hazel, and yet now they fell, almost instantly. When they disappeared beyond the white poplars and willows, I went all tense waiting for the crash. But there were no flames or clouds of smoke. The lake swallowed them up without a sound. Years later we pulled them out. Big Dick, one of the airplanes was called and the other Lady Loreley. The two pilots, Flight Lieutenants Russel P. Judd from Versailles, Kentucky, and Louis S. Davies from Athens, Georgia, or what bits and bones had remained of them, were buried here in the grounds.

After I had taken my leave of William Hazel I walked for a good hour along the country road from Somerleyton to Lowestoft, passing Blundeston prison, which rises out of the flatland like a fortified town and keeps within its walls twelve-hundred inmates at any one time. It was already after six in the evening when I reached the outskirts of Lowestoft. Not a living soul was about in the long streets I went through,

and the closer I came to the town centre the more what I saw disheartened me. The last time I had been in Lowestoft was perhaps fifteen years ago, on a June day that I spent on the beach with two children, and I thought I remembered a town that had become something of a backwater but was nonetheless very pleasant; so now, as I walked into Lowestoft, it seemed incomprehensible to me that in such a relatively short period of time the place could have become so run down. Of course I was aware that this decline had been irreversible ever since the economic crises and depressions of the Thirties; but around 1975, when they were constructing the rigs for the North Sea, there were hopes that things might change for the better, hopes that were steadily inflated during the hardline capitalist years of Baroness Thatcher, till in due course they collapsed in a fever of speculation. The damage spread slowly at first, smouldering underground, and then caught like wildfire. The wharves and factories closed down one after the other, until all that might be said for Lowestoft was that it occupied the easternmost point in the British Isles. Nowadays, in some of the streets almost every other house is up for sale; factory owners, shopkeepers and private individuals are sliding ever deeper into debt; week in, week out, some bankrupt or unemployed person hangs himself; nearly a quarter of the population is now practically illiterate; and there is no sign of an end to the encroaching misery. Although I knew all of this, I was unprepared for the feeling of wretchedness that instantly seized hold of me in Lowestoft, for it is one thing to read about unemployment blackspots in the newspapers and quite another to walk, on a cheerless evening, past rows of run-down houses with mean little front gardens; and, having reached the town centre, to find nothing but amusement arcades, bingo halls, betting shops, video stores, pubs that emit a sour reek of beer from their dark doorways, cheap markets, and seedy bed-and-breakfast establishments with names like Ocean Dawn, Beachcomber, Balmoral, or Layla Lorraine. It was difficult to imagine the holidaymakers and commercial travellers who would want to stay there, nor was it easy – as I climbed the steps coated with shiny blue paint up to the entrance – to recognize the Albion as the "hotel on the promenade of a superior description" recommended in my guidebook, which had been published shortly after the turn of the century. I stood for a good while in the empty lobby, and wandered through the public rooms, which were completely deserted even now at the height of the season – if one can speak of a season in Lowestoft – before I happened upon a startled young woman who, after hunting pointlessly through the register on the reception desk, handed me a huge room key attached to a wooden pear. I noticed that she was dressed in the style of the Thirties and that she avoided eye contact; either her gaze remained fixed on the floor or she looked right through me as if I were not there. That evening I was the sole guest in the huge dining room, and it was the same startled person who took my order and shortly afterwards brought me a fish that had doubtless lain entombed in the deep-freeze for years. The breadcrumb armour-plating of the fish had been partly singed by the grill, and the prongs of my fork bent on it. Indeed it was so difficult to penetrate what eventually proved to be nothing but an empty shell that my plate was a hideous mess once the operation was over. The tartare sauce that I had had to squeeze out of a plastic sachet was turned grey by the sooty breadcrumbs, and the fish itself, or what feigned to be fish, lay a sorry wreck among the grass-green peas and the remains of soggy chips that gleamed with fat. I no longer recall how long I sat in that dining room with its gaudy wallpaper before the nervous young woman, who evidently did all the work in the establishment single-handed, scurried out from the thickening shadows in the background to clear the table. She may have appeared the moment I put down my knife and fork, or perhaps an hour had passed; all I can remember are the scarlet blotches which appeared from the neckline of her blouse and crept up her throat as she bent for my plate. When she had flitted away once more I rose and crossed to the semi-circular bay window. Outside was the beach, somewhere between the darkness and the light, and nothing was moving, neither in the air nor on the land nor on the water. Even the white waves rolling in to the sands seemed to me to be motionless.

The following morning, when I left the Albion Hotel with my rucksack over my shoulder, Lowestoft had reawoken to life, under a cloudless sky. Passing the harbour, where dozens of decommissioned and unemployed trawlers rode at their moorings, I headed south through streets that were now congested with traffic and filled with blue petrol fumes. Once, right by Lowestoft Central station, which had not been refurbished since it was built in the nineteenth century, a black hearse decked out with wreaths slid past me amidst the other vehicles. In it sat two earnest-faced undertaker's men, the driver and a co-driver, and behind them, in the loading area, as it were, someone who had but recently departed this life was lying in his coffin, in his Sunday best, his head on a little pillow, his eyelids closed, hands clasped, and the tips of his shoes pointing up. As I gazed after the hearse I thought of that working lad from Tuttlingen, two hundred years ago, who joined the cortège of a seemingly well-known merchant in Amsterdam and then listened with reverence and emotion to the graveside oration although he knew not a word of Dutch. If before then he had marvelled with envy at the tulips and starflowers behind the windows, and at the crates, bales and chests of tea, sugar, spices and rice that arrived in the docks from the faraway East Indies, from now on, when occasionally he wondered why he had acquired so little on his way through the world, he had only to think of the Amsterdam merchant he had escorted on his last journey, of his big house, his splendid ship, and his narrow grave. With this story in my head I made my way out of a town on which the marks of an insidious decay were everywhere apparent, a town which in its heyday had been not only one of the foremost fishing ports in the United Kingdom but also a seaside resort lauded even abroad as "most salubrious". At that time, in the latter half of the nineteenth century, a number of hotels were built on the south bank of the River Waveney, under the direction of Morton Peto. They met all the requirements of London society circles, and, as well as the hotels, pump rooms and pavilions were built, churches and chapels for every denomination, a lending library, a billiard hall, a tea house that resembled a temple, and a tramway with a magnificent terminus. A broad esplanade, avenues, bowling greens, botanical gardens, and sea- and freshwater baths were established, as were associations for the promotion and beautification of Lowestoft. In no time at all, notes a contemporary account, Lowestoft had risen to pride of place in the public esteem, and now possessed every facility requisite for a bathing resort of repute. Anyone who considered the elegance and perfection of the buildings recently constructed along the south beach, the article continued, would doubtless recognize that everything, from the overall plan to the very last detail, had been informed and shaped by the principles of rationality in the most advantageous way. The crowning glory of the enterprise, which was in every respect exemplary, was the new pier, which stretched four hundred yards out into the North Sea and was considered the most beautiful anywhere along the eastern coast of England. The promenade deck was made of African mahogany planking, and the white pier buildings, which were illuminated after nightfall by gas flares, included a reading and music room with tall mirrors around the walls. Every year at the end of September, as my friend Frederick Farrar told me a few months before he died, a charity ball was held there under the patronage of a member of the royal family to mark the close of the regatta. Frederick was born in Lowestoft in 1906 (far too late, as he once observed to me) and grew up there amidst the care and attention of his three sisters Violet, Iris and Rose. Then in early 1914 he was sent to a preparatory school near Flore in Northamptonshire. The great pain of separation, Frederick recalled, was with me for a long time, especially before going to sleep or when I was tidying my things; but one evening at the start of my second year, when we were told to assemble on the west forecourt, this pain was transformed within me into a kind of perverse pride. We were there to hear a patriotic speech from our headmaster, who told us of the just causes and higher significance of the war which had broken out during the school holidays. When he had finished, said Frederick, a junior cadet named Francis Browne, whom I have not forgotten to this day, played the Last Post on a bugle. From 1924 to 1928, at the wish of his father, who was a solicitor in Lowestoft and for a lengthy period also the consul of Denmark and of the Ottoman Empire,

Frederick read law at Cambridge and London, and subsequently, as he once said with a certain horror, spent more than half a century in lawyers' chambers and courtrooms. Since judges in England generally remain in office well into old age, Frederick had only just retired when in 1982 he bought a house in our neighbourhood and devoted himself to breeding rare roses and violets. I need hardly add that the iris was also one of his favourites. In the course of ten years he grew dozens of varieties of these flowers in the garden he had established, with the help of a young boy who came round almost every day to lend him a hand. His garden was one of the loveliest in the whole region, and towards the end of his life, after a stroke had left him very frail, I often sat there with him, listening to tales of Lowestoft and the past. And it was in that garden, one cloudless day in May, that Frederick died; as he was making his morning round, he somehow managed to set fire to his dressing gown with the cigarette lighter he always kept in his pocket. The garden boy found him an hour later, unconscious and with severe burns from head to foot, in a cool, half-shaded place, where the tiny *viola labradorica* with its almost black leaves had spread and established a regular colony. Frederick succumbed to his injuries that same day. At the funeral in the little graveyard at Framingham Earl I could not help thinking of that child bugler Francis Browne, playing into the night in a Northamptonshire schoolyard in the summer of 1914, and the white pier at Lowestoft, which reached out so far into the sea in those days. Frederick had told me that on the evening of the charity ball the common folk, who in the nature of things were not admitted, rowed out to the end of the pier in a hundred or more boats and barges, to watch, from their bobbing, drifting vantage points, as fashionable society swirled to the sound of the orchestra, seemingly borne aloft in a surge of light above the water, which was dark and at that time in early autumn usually swathed in mist. If I now look back at those times, Frederick once said, it is as if I were seeing everything through flowing white veils: the town like a mirage over the water, the seaside villas right down to the shore surrounded by green trees and shrubs, the summer light, and the beach, across which we have just returned from an outing, Father walking ahead with one or two gentlemen whose trousers are rolled up, Mother by herself with a parasol, my sisters with their skirts gathered in one hand, and the servants bringing up the rear with the donkey, between whose panniers I am sitting on my perch. Once, years ago, said Frederick, I even dreamed of that scene, and our family seemed to me like the court of King James II in exile on the coast of The Hague.

III

Three or four miles south of Lowestoft the coastline curves gently into the land. From the footpath that runs along the grassy dunes and low cliffs one can see, at any time of the day or night and at any time of the year, as I have often found, all manner of tent-like shelters made of poles and cordage, sailcloth and oilskin, along the pebble beach. They are strung out in a long line on the margin of the sea, at regular intervals. It is as if the last stragglers of some nomadic people had settled there,

at the outermost limit of the earth, in expectation of the miracle longed for since time immemorial, the miracle which would justify all their erstwhile privations and wanderings. In reality, however, these men camping out under the heavens have not traversed faraway lands and deserts to reach this strand. Rather, they are from the immediate neighbourhood, and have long been in the habit of fishing there and gazing out to the sea as it changes before their eyes. Curious to tell, their number almost always remains more or less the same. If one strikes camp, another soon takes his place; so that over the years, or so it appears, this company of fishermen dozing by day and waking by night never changes, and indeed may go back further than memory can reach. They say it is rare for any of the fishermen to establish contact with his neighbour, for, although they all look eastward and see both the dusk and the dawn coming up over the horizon, and although they are all moved, I imagine, by the same unfathomable feelings, each of them is nonetheless quite alone and dependent on no one but on himself and on the few items of equipment he has with him, such as a penknife, a thermos flask, or the little transistor radio that gives forth a scarcely audible, scratchy sound, as if the pebbles being dragged back by the waves were talking to each other. I do not believe that these men sit by the sea all day and all night so as not to miss the time when the whiting pass, the flounder rise or the cod come in to the shallower waters, as they claim. They just want to be in a place where they have the world behind them, and before them nothing but emptiness. The fact is that today it is almost impossible to catch anything fishing from the beach. The boats in which the fishermen once put out from the shore have vanished, now that fishing no longer affords a living, and the fishermen themselves are dying out. No one is interested in their legacy. Here and there one comes across abandoned boats that are falling apart, and the cables with which they were once hauled ashore are rusting in the salt air. Out on the high seas the fishing continues, at least for the present, though even there the catches are growing smaller, quite apart from the fact that the fish that are landed are often useless for anything but fish-meal. Every year the rivers bear thousands of tons of mercury, cadmium and lead, and mountains of fertilizer and pesticides, out into the North Sea. A substantial proportion of the heavy metals and other toxic substances sink into the waters of the Dogger Bank, where a third of the fish are now born with strange deformities and excrescences. Time and again, off the coast, rafts of poisonous algae are sighted covering many square miles and reaching thirty feet into the deep, in which the creatures of the sea die in shoals. In some of the rarer varieties of plaice, crucian or bream, the females, in a bizarre mutation, are increasingly developing male sexual organs and the ritual patterns of courtship are now no more than a dance of death, the exact opposite of the notion of the wondrous increase and perpetuation of life with which we grew up. It was not without reason that the herring was always a popular didactic model in primary school, the principal emblem, as it were, of the indestructibility of Nature. I well recall one of those flickering short films that teachers could borrow from local film and slide libraries in the Fifties, which showed a trawler from Wilhelmshaven in almost total darkness riding waves that towered to the top of the screen. By night, it appeared, the nets were cast, and by night they were hauled in again. Everything happened as if in a black void, relieved only by the gleam of the white underbellies of the fish, piled high on the deck, and of the salt they were mixed with. In my memory of that school film I see men in their shining black oilskins working heroically as the angry sea crashes over them time upon time – herring fishing regarded as a supreme example of mankind's struggle with the power of Nature. Towards the end, as the boat is approaching its home port, the rays of the evening sun break through the clouds, spreading their glow over the now becalmed waters. One of the seamen, washed and combed, plays on a mouth organ. The captain, with the air of a man mindful of his responsibilities, stands at the helm, looking ahead into the distance. At last the catch is unloaded and we see the work in the halls where women's hands gut the herring, sort them according to size, and pack them in barrels. Then (so says the booklet accompanying the 1936 film), the railway goods wagons take in this restless wanderer of the seas and transport it to those places where its fate on this earth will at last be fulfilled. I have read elsewhere, in a volume on the natural history of the North Sea

published in Vienna in 1857, that untold millions of herring rise from the lightless depths in the spring and summer months, to spawn in coastal waters and shallows, where they lie one on top of another in layers. And a statement ending with an exclamation mark informs us that each female herring lays seventy thousand eggs, which, according to Buffon's calculation, would shortly produce a volume of fish twenty times the size of the earth, if they were all to develop unhindered. Indeed, the records note years in which the entire herring fisheries threatened to go under, beneath a truly catastrophic glut of herring. It is even said that vast shoals of herring were brought in towards the beaches by the wind and the tides and cast ashore, covering miles of the coast to a depth of two feet and more. The local people were able to salvage only a small portion of these herring harvests in baskets and crates; the remainder rotted within days, affording the terrible sight of Nature suffocating on its own surfeit. On the other hand, there were repeated occasions when the herring avoided their usual grounds and whole stretches of coastline were impoverished as a result. The routes the herring take through the sea have not been ascertained to this day. It has been supposed that variations in the level of light and the prevailing winds influence the course of their wanderings, or geomagnetic fields, or the shifting marine isotherms, but none of these speculations has proved verifiable. For this reason, those who go in pursuit of herring have always relied on their traditional knowledge, which draws upon legend, and is based on their own observation of facts such as the tendency of the fish, swimming in even, wedge-shaped formations, to reflect a pulsating glow skyward when the sunlight falls at a particular angle. One dependable sign that herring are present is said to be myriads of scales floating on the surface of the water, shimmering like tiny silver tiles by day and sometimes at dusk resembling ashes or snow. Once the herring shoal had been sighted, it was fished during the following night, and this was done, according to the natural history of the North Sea already quoted, using nets two hundred feet long that could take almost a quarter of a million fish. These nets were made of coarse Persian silk and dyed black, since experience had shown that a lighter colour scared the herring off. The nets do not enclose the catch, but rather present a kind of wall in the water which the fish swim up against in desperation until at length their gills catch in the mesh; they are then throttled during the near-eight-hour process of hauling up and winding in the nets. Because of this, by far the majority of the herrings are lifeless by the time they are hoisted out of the water. Earlier natural historians such as M. de Lacépède therefore tended to suppose that herring die the instant they are removed from water, from some form of infarct or other cause. Since all authorities were soon agreed in ascribing this particular characteristic to the herring, much attention was long paid to eye-witness accounts of herrings remaining alive out of the water. Thus it is recorded that a Canadian missionary by the name of Pierre Sagard watched a batch of herring thrashing about for some time on the deck of a fishing boat off the Newfoundland coast, and that one Herr Neucrantz of Stralsund meticulously chronicled the final throes of a herring that had been taken from the water one hour and seven minutes before the time of its death. Again, the inspector of the Rouen fish market, a certain Noel de Marinière, one day saw to his astonishment that a pair of herring that had already been out of the water between two and three hours were still moving, a circumstance that prompted him to investigate more closely the fishes' capacity to survive, which he did by cutting off their fins and mutilating them in other ways. This process, inspired by our thirst for knowledge, might be described as the most extreme of the sufferings undergone by a species always threatened by disaster. What is not eaten at the spawn stage by haddock and sucker fish ends up inside a conger eel, dogfish, cod or one of the many others that prey on herring, including, not least, ourselves. As early as 1670, more than eight hundred thousand Dutch and Friesians, a not inconsiderable part of the entire population, were employed in herring fishing. A hundred years later, the number of herring caught annually is estimated to have been sixty billion. Given these quantities, the natural historians sought consolation in the idea that humanity was responsible for only a fraction of the endless destruction wrought in the cycle of life, and moreover in the assumption that the peculiar physiology of the fish left them free of the fear and pains that rack the bodies and souls of higher animals in their death throes. But the truth is that we do not know what the herring feels. All we know is that its internal structure is extremely intricate and consists of more than two hundred different bones and cartilages.

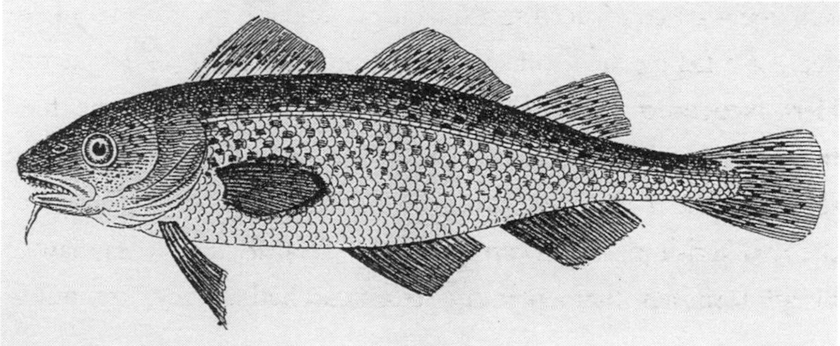

Among the herring's most striking external features are its powerful tail fin, the narrow head, the slightly prominent lower mandible, and its large eye, with a black pupil swimming in the silvery-white iris. The herring's dorsal area is of a bluish-green colour. The individual scales on its flanks and belly shimmer a golden orange, but taken together they present a metallic, pure white gleam. Held against the light, the rearward parts of the fish appear a dark green of a beauty one sees nowhere else. Once the life has fled the herring, its colours change. Its back turns blue, the cheeks and gills red, suffused with blood. An idiosyncrasy peculiar to the herring is that, when dead, it begins to glow; this property, which resembles phosphorescence and is yet altogether different, peaks a few days after death and then ebbs away as the fish decays. For a long time no one could account for this glowing of the lifeless herring, and indeed I believe that it still remains unexplained. Around 1870, when projects for the total illumination of our cities were everywhere afoot, two English scientists with the

apt names of Herrington and Lightbown investigated the unusual phenomenon in the hope that the luminous substance exuded by dead herrings would lead to a formula for an organic source of light that had the capacity to regenerate itself. The failure of this eccentric undertaking, as I read some time ago in a history of artificial light, constituted no more than a negligible setback in the relentless conquest of darkness.

I had long left the beach fishermen behind me when, in the early afternoon, I reached Benacre Broad, a lake of brackish water beyond a bank of shingle halfway between Lowestoft and Southwold. The lake is encircled by deciduous woodland that is now dying, owing to the steady erosion of the coastline by the sea. Doubtless it is only a matter of time before one stormy night the shingle bank is broken, and the appearance of the entire area changes. But that day, as I sat on the tranquil shore, it was possible to believe one was gazing into eternity. The veils of mist that drifted inland that morning had cleared, the vault of the sky was empty and blue, not the slightest breeze was stirring, the trees looked painted, and not a single bird flew across the velvet-brown water. It was as if the world were under a bell jar, until great cumulus clouds brewed up out of the west casting a grey shadow upon the earth.

Perhaps it was that darkening that called to my mind an article I had clipped from the *Eastern Daily Press* several months before, on the death of Major George Wyndham Le Strange, whose great stone manor house in Henstead stood beyond the lake. During the last War, the report read, Le Strange served in the anti-tank regiment that liberated the camp at Bergen Belsen on the 14th of April 1945,

but immediately after VE-Day returned home from Germany to manage his great uncle's estates in Suffolk, a task he had fulfilled in exemplary manner, at least until the mid-Fifties, as I knew from other sources. It was at that time too that Le Strange took on the housekeeper to whom he eventually left his entire fortune: his estates in Suffolk as well as property in the centre of Birmingham estimated at several million pounds. According to the newspaper report, Le Strange employed this housekeeper, a simple young woman from Beccles by the name of Florence Barnes, on the explicit condition that she take the meals she prepared together with him, but in absolute silence. Mrs Barnes told the newspaper herself that she abided by this arrangement, once made, even when her employer's way of life became increasingly odd. Though Mrs Barnes gave only the most reticent of responses to the reporter's enquiries, my own subsequent investigations revealed that in the late Fifties Le Strange discharged his household staff and his labourers, gardeners and administrators one after another, that thenceforth he lived alone in the great stone house with the silent cook from Beccles, and that as a result the whole estate, with its gardens and park, became overgrown and neglected, while scrub and undergrowth encroached on the fallow fields. Apart from comments that touched upon these matters of fact, stories concerning the Major himself were in circulation in the villages that bordered on his domain, stories to which one can lend only a limited credence. They drew, I imagine, on the little that reached the outside world over the years, rumours from the depths of the estate that occupied the people who lived in the immediate vicinity. Thus in a Henstead hostelry, for example, I

EDP [illegible]

Housekeeper Rewarded for Silent Dinners

A wealthy eccentric has left his vast estate to the housekeeper to whom he hardly spoke for over thirty years.

Major George Wyndham Le Strange (77), a bachelor, collapsed and died last month in the hallway of his manor house in Henstead, Suffolk which had remained virtually unchanged since Georgian times.

During the last war, Le Strange had served in the 63rd Anti-Tank Regiment which liberated the concentration camp at Belsen on 14 April 1945. Immediately after VE-Day, he returned to Suffolk to manage his great uncle's estates.

Mrs. Florence Barnes (57), employed by Le Strange in 1955 as housekeeper and cook on condition that she dined with him in silence every day, said that Le Strange had, in the course of time, become a virtual recluse but she refused to give any details of the Major's eccentric way of life.

Asked about her inheritance, she said that, beyond wanting to buy a bungalow in Beccles for herself and her sister, she had no idea what to do with it.

heard it said that in his old age, since he had worn out his wardrobe and saw no point in buying new clothes, Le Strange would wear garments dating from bygone days which he fetched out of chests in the attic as he needed them. There were people who claimed to have seen him on occasion dressed in a canary-yellow frock coat or a kind of mourning robe of faded violet taffeta with numerous buttons and eyes. Le Strange, who had always kept a tame cockerel in his room, was reputed to have been surrounded, in later years, by all manner of feathered creatures: by guinea fowl, pheasants, pigeons and quail, and various kinds of garden and song birds, strutting about him on the floor or flying around in the air. Some said that one summer Le Strange dug a cave in his garden and sat in it day and night like St Jerome in the desert. Most curious of all was a legend that I presume to have originated with the Wrentham undertaker's staff, to the effect that the Major's pale skin was olive-green when he passed away, his goose-grey eye was pitch-dark, and his snow-white hair had turned to raven-black. To this day I do not know what to make of such stories. One thing is certain: the estate and all its adjunct properties was bought at auction by a Dutchman last autumn, and Florence Barnes, the Major's loyal housekeeper, lives now with her sister Jemima in a bungalow in her home town of Beccles, as she had intended.

A quarter of an hour's walk south of Benacre Broad, where the beach narrows and a stretch of sheer coastline begins, a few dozen dead trees lie in a confused heap where they fell years ago from the Covehithe cliffs. Bleached by salt water, wind and sun, the broken, barkless wood looks like the bones of some extinct species, greater even than the mammoths and dinosaurs, that came to grief long since on this solitary strand. The footpath leads around the tangle, through a bank of gorse, up to the loamy cliff-head, and there it continues amidst bracken, the tallest of which stood as high as my shoulder, not far from the ledge, which is constantly threatening to crumble away. Out on the leaden-coloured sea a sailing boat kept me company, or rather, it seemed to me as if it were motionless and I myself, step by step, were making as little progress as

that invisible spirit aboard his unmoving barque. But by degrees the bracken thinned, affording a view of a field that extended as far as Covehithe church. Beyond a low electric fence lay a herd of almost a hundred head of swine, on brown earth where meagre patches of camomile grew. I climbed over the wire and approached one of the ponderous, immobile, sleeping animals. As I bent towards it, it opened a small eye fringed with light lashes and gave me an enquiring look. I ran my hand across its dusty back, and it trembled at this unwonted touch; I stroked its snout and face, and chucked it in the hollow behind one ear, till at length it sighed like one enduring endless suffering. When I stood up, it closed its eye once more with an expression of profound submissiveness. For a while I sat on the grass between the electric fence and the cliff edge. The thin, yellowing blades of grass were bending in the rising wind. The sky was darkening as banks of cloud were piling far out across the sea, which was now streaked with white. All of a sudden, the boat, which for so long had not moved, was gone. The scene reminded me of the story St Mark the evangelist tells, of the country of the Gadarenes, which follows the far better-known account of the calming of the storm on the Sea of Galilee. Neatly as the image of the doubting disciples waking their master from his untroubled sleep when the waves beat into the ship fitted the school catechism, there was little understanding of what the story of the mad Gadarene meant. I at least could not recall its ever being read to us in our so-called religious knowledge lessons or at church, much less explained. The raging maniac, of whom it is said that he came out of the tombs where he dwelt, was possessed of so violent an unclean spirit that he could not be bound or tamed. He plucked asunder the chains, and broke the fetters in pieces. Always he was in the mountains, writes St Mark, and in the tombs, crying, and cutting himself with stones. Asked his name, he answered: My name is Legion: for we are many. And he besought the Lord not to send him away out of the country. But the Lord commanded the unclean spirits to enter the herd of swine feeding there. And the swine, some two thousand according to the evangelist, plunged down a steep slope and drowned in the sea. Is this terrible story, I asked myself, as I sat overlooking the German Ocean, the report of a credible witness? If so, does that not mean that in healing the Gadarene Our Lord committed a serious error of judgment? Or was this parable made up by the evangelist, I wondered, to explain the supposed uncleanliness of swine; which would imply that human reasoning, diseased as it is, needs to seize on some other kind that it can take to be inferior and thus deserving of annihilation? As these things were going through my mind I was watching the sand martins darting to and fro over the sea. Ceaselessly emitting their tiny cries, they sped along their flight-paths faster than my eyes could follow them. At earlier times, in the summer evenings during my childhood when I had watched from the valley as swallows circled in the last light, still in great numbers in those days, I would imagine that the world was held together by the courses they flew through the air. Many years later, in *Tlön, Uqbar, Orbis Tertius*, which was written in 1940 at Salto Oriental in Uruguay, I read of how a few birds saved an entire amphitheatre. The sand martins, I now saw, were flying solely at the level that extended from the top of the cliff where I was sitting out into empty space. Not one of them climbed higher or dived lower, to the water below them. Whenever they came towards me, fast as bullets, some seemed to vanish right beneath my feet, as if into the very ground. I went to the edge of the cliff and saw that they had dug their nesting holes into the topmost layer of clay, one beside the other. I was thus standing on perforated ground, as it were, which might have given way at any moment. Nevertheless, I laid my head back as far as I could, as I did as a boy for a dare on the flat tin roof of the two-storey apiary, fixed my eyes on the zenith, then lowered my gaze till it met the horizon, and drew it in across the water, to the narrow strip of beach some twenty yards below. As I tried to suppress the mounting sense of dizziness, breathing out and taking a step backwards, I thought I saw something of an odd, pallid colour move on the shoreline. I crouched down and, overcome by a sudden panic, looked over the edge. A couple lay down there, in the bottom of the pit, as I thought: a man stretched full length over another body of which nothing was visible but the legs, spread and angled. In the startled moment when that image went through me, which lasted an eternity, it seemed as if the man's feet twitched like those of one just hanged. Now, though, he lay still, and the woman too was still and motionless. Misshapen, like some great mollusc washed ashore, they lay there, to all appearances a single being, a many-limbed, two-headed monster that had drifted in from far out at sea, the last of a prodigious species, its life ebbing from it with each breath expired through its nostrils. Filled with consternation, I stood up once more, shaking as if it were the first time in my life that I had got to my feet, and left the place, which seemed fear-some to me now, taking the path that descended from the cliff-top to where the beach spread out on the southerly side. Far off in front of me lay Southwold, a cluster of distant buildings, clumps of trees, and a snow-white lighthouse, beneath a dark sky. Before I reached the town, the first drops of rain were falling. I turned to look back down the deserted stretch I had come by, and could no longer have said whether I had really seen the pale sea monster at the foot of the Covehithe cliffs or whether I had imagined it.

Recalling the uncertainty I then felt brings me back to the Argentinian tale I have referred to before, a tale which deals with our attempts to invent secondary or tertiary worlds. The narrator describes dining with Adolfo Bioy Casares in a house in Calle Gaona in Ramos Mejìa one evening in 1935. He relates that after dinner they had a long and rambling talk about the writing of a novel that would fly in the face of palpable facts and become entangled in contradictions in such a way that few readers – very few readers – would be able to grasp the hidden, horrific, yet at the same time quite meaningless point of the narrative. At the end of the passage that led to the room where we were sitting, the author continues, hung an oval, half-fogged mirror that had a somewhat disquieting effect. We felt that this dumb witness was keeping a watch on us, and thus we discovered – discoveries of this kind are almost always made in the dead of night – that there is something sinister about mirrors. Bioy Casares then recalled the observation of one of the heresiarchs of Uqbar, that the disturbing thing about mirrors, and also the act of copulation, is that they multiply the number of human beings. I asked Bioy Casares for the source of this memorable remark, the author writes, and he told me that it was in the entry on Uqbar in the *Anglo-American Cyclopaedia.* As the story goes on, however, it is revealed that this entry is nowhere to be found in the encyclopaedia in question, or rather, it appears uniquely in the copy bought years earlier by Bioy Casares, the twenty-sixth volume of which contains four pages that are not in any other copy of the edition in question, that of 1917. It thus remains unclear whether Uqbar ever existed or whether the description of this unknown country might not be a case similar to that of Tlön, the encyclopaedists' project to which the main portion of the narrative in question is devoted and which aimed at creating a new reality, in the course of time, by way of the unreal. The labyrinthine construction of Tlön, reads a note added to the text in 1947, is on the point of blotting out the known world. The language of Tlön, which hitherto no one had mastered, has now invaded the academies; already the history of Tlön has superseded all that we formerly knew or thought we knew; in historiography, the indisputable advantages of a fictitious past have become apparent. Almost every branch of learning has been reformed. A ramified dynasty of hermits, the dynasty of the Tlön inventors, encyclopaedists and lexicographers, has changed the face of the earth. Every language, even Spanish, French and English, will disappear from the planet. The world will be Tlön. But, the narrator concludes, what is that to me? In the peace and quiet of my country villa I continue to hone my tentative translation, schooled on Quevedo, of Thomas Browne's *Urn Burial* (which I do not mean to publish).

IV

The rain clouds had dispersed when, after dinner, I took my first walk around the streets and lanes of the town. Darkness was falling, and only the lighthouse with its shining glass cabin still caught the last luminous rays that came in from the western horizon.

Footsore and weary as I was after my long walk from Lowestoft, I sat down on a bench on the green called Gunhill and looked out on the tranquil sea, from the depths of which the shadows were now rising. Everyone who had been out for an evening stroll was gone. I felt as if I were in a deserted theatre, and I should not have been surprised if a curtain had suddenly risen before me and on the proscenium I had beheld, say, the 28th of May 1672 – that memorable day when the Dutch fleet appeared offshore from out of the drifting mists, with the bright morning light behind it, and opened fire on the English ships in Sole Bay. In all likelihood the people of Southwold hurried out of the town as soon as the first cannonades were fired to watch the rare spectacle from the beach. Shading their eyes with their hands against the dazzling sun, they would have watched the ships moving hither and thither, apparently at random, their sails billowing in a light north-east wind and then, as they manoeuvred ponderously, flapping once again. They would not have been able to make out human figures at that distance, not even the gentlemen of the Dutch and English admiralties on the bridges. As the battle continued, the powder magazines exploded, and some of the tarred hulls burned down to the waterline; the scene would have been shrouded in an acrid, yellowish-black smoke creeping across the entire bay and masking the combat from view. While most of the accounts of the battles fought on the so-called fields of honour have from time immemorial been unreliable, the pictorial representations of great naval engagements are without exception figments of the imagination. Even celebrated painters such as Storck, van der Velde or de Loutherbourg, some of whose versions of the

Battle of Sole Bay I studied closely in the Maritime Museum in Greenwich, fail to convey any true impression of how it must have been to be on board one of these ships, already overloaded with equipment and men, when burning masts and sails began to fall or cannonballs smashed into the appallingly overcrowded decks.

On the Royal James alone, which was set aflame by a fireship, nearly half the thousand-strong crew perished. No details of the end of the three-master have come down to us. There were eye-witnesses who claimed to have seen the commander of the English fleet, the Earl of Sandwich, who weighed almost twenty-four stone, gesticulating on the afterdeck as the flames encircled him. All we know for certain is that his bloated body was washed up on the beach near Harwich a few weeks later. The seams of his uniform had burst asunder, the buttonholes were torn open, yet the Order of the Garter still gleamed in undiminished splendour.

At that date there can have been only a few cities on earth that numbered as many souls as were annihilated in sea-battles of this kind. The agony that was endured and the enormity of the havoc wrought defeat our powers of comprehension, just as we cannot conceive the vastness of the effort that must have been required – from felling and preparing the timber, mining and smelting the ore, and forging the iron, to weaving and sewing the sailcloth – to build and equip vessels that were almost all predestined for destruction. For a brief time only these curious creatures sailed the seas, moved by the winds that circle the earth, bearing names such as Stavoren, Resolution, Victory, Groot Hollandia and Olyfan, and then they were gone. It has never been determined, which of the two parties in the naval battle fought off Southwold to extort trading advantages emerged victorious. It is certain, however, that the decline of the Netherlands began here, with a shift in the balance of power so small that it was out of proportion to the human and material resources expended in the battle; while on the other hand the English government, almost bankrupt, diplomatically isolated, and humiliated by the Dutch raid on Chatham, was now able, despite a complete absence of strategic thinking and a naval administration on the verge of disintegration, and thanks only to the vagaries of the wind and the waves that day, to commence the sovereignty at sea that was to be unbroken for so long. – As I sat there that evening in Southwold overlooking the German Ocean, I sensed quite clearly the earth's slow turning into the dark. The huntsmen are up in America, writes Thomas Browne in *The Garden of Cyrus*, and they are already past their first sleep in Persia. The shadow of night is drawn like a black veil across the earth, and since almost all creatures, from one meridian to the next, lie down after the sun has set, so, he continues, one might, in following the setting sun, see on our globe nothing but prone bodies, row upon row, as if levelled by the scythe of Saturn – an endless graveyard for a humanity struck by falling sickness. I gazed farther and farther out to sea, to where the darkness was thickest and where there extended a cloudbank of the most curious shape, which I could barely make out any longer, the rearward view, I presume, of the storm that had broken over Southwold in the late afternoon. For a while, the topmost summit regions of this massif, dark as ink, glistened like the icefields of the Caucasus, and as I watched the glare fade I remembered that years before, in a dream, I had once walked the entire length of a mountain range just as remote and just as unfamiliar. It must have been a distance of a thousand miles or more, through ravines, gorges and valleys, across ridges, slopes and drifts, along the edges of great forests, over wastes of rock, shale and snow. And I recalled that in my dream, once I had reached the end of my journey, I looked back, and that it was six o'clock in the evening. The jagged peaks of the mountains I had left behind rose in almost fearful silhouette against a turquoise sky in which two or three pink clouds drifted. It was a scene that felt familiar in an inexplicable way, and for weeks it was on my mind until at length I realized that, down to the last detail, it matched the Vallüla massif, which I had seen from the bus, through eyes drooping with tiredness, a day or so before I started school, as we returned home from an outing to the Montafon. I suppose it is submerged memories that give to dreams their curious air of hyper-reality. But perhaps there is something else as well, something nebulous, gauze-like, through which everything one sees in a dream seems, paradoxically, much clearer. A pond becomes a lake, a breeze becomes a storm, a handful of dust is a desert, a grain of sulphur in the blood is a volcanic inferno. What manner of theatre is it, in which we are at once playwright, actor, stage manager, scene painter and audience?

Just as these things have always been beyond my understanding, so too I found it impossible to believe, as I sat on Gunhill in Southwold that evening, that just one year earlier I had been looking across to England from a beach in Holland. On that occasion, following a bad night spent at Baden in Switzerland, I had travelled via Basle and Amsterdam to The Hague, where I had taken a room in one of the less salubrious hotels near the station. I no longer remember whether it was the Lord Asquith, the Aristo, or the Fabiola. At all events, in the lobby of this establishment, which would deeply have depressed even the humblest of travellers, there sat two gentlemen, no longer in their first youth, who must have been partners for a long time; and between them, in the stead of a child, as it were, was an apricot-coloured poodle. After I had rested a little in the room I was allotted, I went for a stroll, looking for a bite to eat, up the road that runs from the station to the city centre, past the Bristol Bar, Yuksel's Café, a videoboetiek, Aran Turk's pizza place, a Euro-sex-shop, a halal butcher's, and a carpet store, above whose display a rudimentary fresco in four parts showed a caravan crossing the desert. The name Perzenpaleis was lettered in red on the façade of the run-down building, the upper-storey windows of which were all white-washed over.

As I was looking up at this façade, a man with a dark beard, wearing a suit jacket over a long tunic, slipped past me through a doorway, so close that our elbows touched. Through that doorway, for an unforgettable moment that seemed to exist outside time, I glimpsed the wooden rack on which perhaps a hundred pairs of well-worn shoes had been placed beside and above one another. Only later did I see the minaret rising from the courtyard of the building into the azure Dutch evening sky. For an hour or more I walked around this somehow extraterritorial part of town. Most of the windows in the side streets were boarded up, and slogans like Help de regenwouden redden or Welcome to the Royal Dutch Graveyard were graffiti'd on the sooty brick walls. No longer able to decide on a place to eat, I bought a carton of chips at McDonald's, where I felt like a criminal wanted worldwide as I stood at the brightly lit counter, and ate them as I walked back to my hotel. Outside the entrances of the entertainment and dining establishments on the road to the station, small groups of oriental men had now gathered, most of them smoking in silence while the odd one appeared to be doing a deal with a client. When I reached the little canal that crosses the road, an open-top American limousine studded with lights and gleaming with chrome glided past me across the carriageway as if it had come out of nowhere, and in it sat a pimp in a white suit, wearing gold-framed sunglasses and on his head a ludicrous Tyrolean hat. And as I stood gazing in amazement after this almost supernatural apparition, a dark-skinned man shot round the corner towards me, sheer terror in his face, and, swerving to avoid me, left me full in the path of his pursuer, who, judging by appearances, was a country-man of his. This pursuer, whose eyes were shining with rage and blood lust, was probably a chef or kitchen porter, since he was wearing an apron and holding a long, glinting knife in one hand, which passed by me so close that I imagined I felt it piercing between my ribs. Disturbed by the impression this experience made on me, I lay on my bed in my hotel room. I did not have a good night. It was so oppressive and sultry that one could not leave the windows closed; but if one opened them, one heard the din of traffic from the crossroads and every few minutes the dreadful squeal of the tram as it ground round the terminus track-loop. I was therefore not in the best of states next morning at the Mauritshuis when I stood before the large group portrait, *The Anatomy Lesson.* Although I had gone to The Hague especially to see this painting, which would continue to occupy me considerably over the years to come, I was so out of sorts after my bad night that I was quite unable to harness my thoughts as I looked at the body being dissected under the eyes of the Guild of Surgeons. Indeed, without knowing why, I was so affected by the painting that later it took me a full hour to recover, in front of Jacob van Ruisdael's *View of Haarlem with Bleaching Fields*. The flatland stretching out towards Haarlem is seen from above, from a vantage point generally identified as the dunes, though the sense of a bird's-eye view is so strong that the dunes would have to be veritable hills or even modest mountains. The truth is of course that Ruisdael did not take up a position on the dunes in order to paint; his vantage point was an imaginary position some distance above the earth. Only in this way could he see it all together: the vast cloudscape that occupies two thirds of the picture; the town, which is little more than a fraying of the horizon, except for St Bavo's cathedral, which towers above all the other buildings; the dark bosks and bushes; the farm in the foreground; and the bright field where the sheets of white linen have been laid out to bleach and where, by my count, seven or eight people no taller than a quarter of an inch, are going about their work. After I left the gallery, I sat for a while on the sunlit steps of the palais which Governor Johann Maurits, as the guidebook I had bought informed me, had built in his homeland whilst he was in Brazil for seven years, and fitted out as a cosmographic residence reflecting the wonders of the remotest regions of the earth, in keeping with his personal motto: "Even unto the limits of our world". Report has it that when the house was opened in May 1644, three hundred years before I was born, eleven Indians the Governor had brought with him from Brazil performed a dance on the cobbled square in front of the new building, conveying to the townspeople some sense of the foreign lands to which the power of their community now extended. These dancers, about whom nothing else is known, have long since disappeared, as soundless as shadows, as silent as the heron I saw when I set off once more, flying just above the shining surface of the water, the beat of its wings calm and even, undisturbed by the traffic creeping along the bank of the Hofvijver. Who can say how things were in ages past? Diderot, in one of his travel journals, described Holland as the Egypt of Europe, where one might cross the fields in a boat and, as far as the eye could see, there would be scarcely anything to break the flooded surface of the plain. In that curious country, he wrote, the most modest rise gave one the loftiest sensation. And for Diderot there was nothing more satisfying to the human mind than the neat Dutch towns with their straight, tree-lined canals, exemplary in every respect. Settlement succeeded settlement just as if they had been conjured up overnight by the hand of an artist in accordance with some carefully worked-out plan, wrote Diderot, and even in the heart of the largest of them one still felt one was out in the country. The Hague, at that time with a population of about forty thousand, he felt was the loveliest village on earth, and the road from the town to the strand at Scheveningen a promenade without equal. It was not easy to appreciate these observations as I walked along Parkstraat towards Scheveningen. Here and there stood a fine villa in its garden, but otherwise there was nothing to afford me any respite. Perhaps I had gone the wrong way, as so often in unfamiliar cities. In Scheveningen, where I had hoped to be able to see the sea from a distance, I walked for a long time in the shadow of tall apartment blocks, as if at the bottom of a ravine. When at last I reached the beach I was so tired that I lay down and slept till the afternoon. I heard the surge of the sea, and, half dreaming, understood every word of Dutch and for the first time in my life believed I had arrived, and was home. Even when I awoke it seemed to me for a moment that my people were resting all around me as we made our way across the desert. The façade of the Kurhaus towered above me like a great caravanserai, a comparison which sat well with the fact

that the palatial hotel, built on the beach at the turn of the century, had numerous modern extensions with roofs resembling tents, housing newsagents, souvenir shops and fast-food outlets. In one of these, the Massada Grill, where the illuminated photo-panels above the counter showed kosher foods instead of the usual hamburger combinations, I had a cup of tea before returning to the city and marvelled at a beatifically beaming couple surrounded by the motley host of their grandchildren, celebrating some family or holiday occasion in a cafeteria otherwise deserted.

That evening, in Amsterdam, I sat in the peace of the lounge of a private hotel by the Vondel Park, which I knew from earlier visits, and made notes on the stations of my journey, now almost at an end: the days I had spent on various enquiries at Bad Kissingen, the panic attack in Baden, the boat excursion on Lake Zurich, my run of good luck at the casino in Lindau, and my visits to the Alte Pinakothek in Munich and to the grave of my patron saint in Nuremberg, of whom legend has it that he was the son of a king, from Dacia or Denmark, who married a French princess in Paris. During the wedding night, the story goes, he was afflicted with a sense of profound unworthiness. Today, he is supposed to have said to his bride, our bodies are adorned, but tomorrow they will be food for worms. Before the break of day, he fled, making a pilgrimage to Italy, where he lived in solitude until he felt the power to work miracles arising within him. After saving the Anglo-Saxon princes Winnibald and Wunibald from certain starvation with a loaf baked from ashes and brought to them by a celestial messenger, and after preaching a celebrated sermon in Vicenza, he went over the Alps to Germany. At Regensburg he crossed the Danube on his cloak, and there made a broken glass whole again; and, in the house of a wheelwright too mean to spare the kindling, lit a fire with icicles. This story of the burning of the frozen substance of life has, of late, meant much to me, and I wonder now whether inner coldness and desolation may not be the pre-condition for making the world believe, by a kind of fraudulent showmanship, that one's own wretched heart is still aglow. Be that as it may, my namesake is said to have performed many more miracles in his hermitage in the imperial forests between the rivers Regnitz and Pegnitz, and to have healed the sick, before his corpse, as he had ordained, was borne on a cart drawn by two oxen to the place where his grave is to this day.

Centuries later, in May 1507, the Patriciate of Nuremberg resolved to have a brass sarcophagus crafted for the holy prince of heaven St Sebolt by master smith Peter Vischer. In June 1519, when his twelve-year labours were completed, the great monument, weighing many tons, standing almost five yards high on twelve snails and four curved dolphins, and representing the entire order of salvation,

was installed in the chancel of the church consecrated in the name of the city's saint. On the base of the tomb, fauns, mermaids, fabulous creatures and animals of every conceivable description throng about the four cardinal virtues of Justice, Prudence, Temperance and Fortitude. Above them are mythical figures – Nimrod the hunter, Hercules with his club, Samson with the jawbone of an ass, and the god Apollo between two swans – along with representations of the miracle of the burning of ice, the feeding of the hungry, and the conversion of a heretic. Then come the apostles with their emblems and the instruments of their martyrdom, and, crowning all, the celestial city with its three pinnacles and many mansions, Jerusalem, the fervently longed-for bride, God's tabernacle amongst mankind, the image of an other, renewed life. And in the heart of this reliquary cast in a single piece, surrounded by eighty angels, in a shrine of sheet silver, lie the bones of the exemplary dead man, the harbinger of a time when the tears will be wiped from our eyes and there will be no more grief, or pain, or weeping and wailing.

Night had fallen and I sat in the darkness of my room on the top floor of the Vondel Park Hotel and listened to the stormy gusts buffeting the crowns of the trees. From afar came the rumble of thunder. Pallid sheet lightning streaked the horizon. At about one o'clock, when I heard the first drops rattling on the metal roof, I leant out of the window into the warm, storm-filled air. Soon the rain was pouring down into the shadowy depths of the park, which flared from time to time as if lit up by Bengal fire. The water in the gutter gurgled like a mountain stream. Once, when lightning again flashed across the sky, I looked down into the hotel garden far below me, and there, in the broad ditch that runs between the garden and the park, in the shelter of an overhanging willow, I saw a solitary mallard, motionless on the garish green surface of the water. This image emerged from the darkness, for a fraction of a second, with such perfect clarity that I can still see every individual willow leaf, the myriad green scales of duckweed, the subtlest nuances in the fowl's plumage, and even the pores in the lid closed over its eye.

Next morning, the atmosphere at Schiphol airport was so strangely muted that one might have thought one was already a good way beyond this world. As if they were under sedation or moving through time stretched and expanded, the passengers wandered the halls or, standing still on the escalators, were delivered to their various destinations on high or underground. In the train from Amsterdam, leafing through Lévi-Strauss's *Tristes Tropiques*, I had come across a description of the Campos Elyseos, a street in São Paulo where the colourfully painted wooden villas and residences, built at the turn of the century by the wealthy in a kind of Swiss fantasy style, were falling to pieces in gardens overgrown with eucalyptus and mango trees. Perhaps that was why the airport, filled with a murmuring whisper, seemed to me that morning like an ante room of that undiscovered country from whose bourn no traveller returns. Every now and then the announcers' voices, disembodied and intoning their messages like angels, would call someone's name. Passagiers Sandberg en Stromberg naar Copenhagen. Mr Freeman to Lagos. La señora Rodrigo, por favor. Sooner or later the call would come for each and every one of those waiting here. I sat down on one of the upholstered benches where travellers who had spent the night in this place of transit were still asleep, stretched out unconscious or curled up. Not far from me was a group of Africans, clad in flowing, snow-white robes; and opposite me a well-groomed gentleman with a golden fob-chain crossing his waistcoat was reading a newspaper, on the front page of which was a photograph of a vast pall of smoke, boiling up like an atomic mushroom cloud above an atoll. De aswolk boven de vulkaan Pinatubo read the headline. Outside, on the tarmac, the summer heat was shimmering, tiny trucks were beetling to and fro, and from the runway aeroplanes with hundreds of people aboard rose, one after another into the blue air. For my part, I must have dozed off for a while as I watched this spectacle, because presently I heard my name from afar, followed by the injunction Immediate boarding at Gate C4 please.

The small propeller plane that services the route from Amsterdam to Norwich first climbed toward the sun before turning west. Spread out beneath us lay one of the most densely-populated regions in Europe, with endless terraces, sprawling satellite towns, business parks and shining glass houses which looked like large quadrangular ice floes drifting across this corner of the continent where not a patch is left to its own devices. Over the centuries the land had been regulated, cultivated and built on until the whole region was transformed into a geometrical pattern. The roads, water channels and railway tracks ran in straight lines and gentle curves past fields and plantations, basins and reservoirs. Like beads on an abacus designed to calculate infinity, cars glided along the lanes of the motorways, while the ships moving up and down river appeared as if they had been halted for ever. Embedded in this even fabric lay a manor surrounded by its park, the relic of an earlier age. I watched the shadow of our plane hastening below us across hedges and fences, rows of poplars and canals. Along a line that seemed to have been drawn with a ruler a tractor crawled through a field of stubble, dividing it into one lighter and one darker half. Nowhere, however, was a single human being to be seen. No matter whether one is flying over Newfoundland or the sea of lights that stretches from Boston to Philadelphia after nightfall, over the Arabian deserts which gleam like mother-of-pearl, over the Ruhr or the city of Frankfurt, it is as though there were no people, only the things they have made and in which they are hiding. One sees the places where they live and the roads that link them, one sees the smoke rising from their houses and factories, one sees the vehicles in which they sit, but one sees not the people themselves. And yet they are present everywhere upon the face of the earth, extending their dominion by the hour, moving around the honeycombs of towering buildings and tied into networks of a complexity that goes far beyond the power of any one individual to imagine, from the thousands of hoists and winches that once worked the South African diamond

mines to the floors of today's stock and commodity exchanges, through which the global tides of information flow without cease. If we view ourselves from a great height, it is frightening to realize how little we know about our species, our purpose and our end, I thought, as we crossed the coastline and flew out over the jelly-green sea.

Such were my reminiscences concerning my visit to Holland a year before, as I sat on Gunhill that evening. Now, with an advancing chill in the air, I sought the familiarity of the streets and soon found myself outside the Sailors' Reading Room, a charitable establishment housed in a small building above the promenade, which nowadays, sailors being a dying breed, serves principally as a kind of maritime museum, where all manner of things connected with the sea and seafaring life are kept and collected. On the walls hang barometers and navigational instruments, figureheads, and models of ships in glass cases and in bottles. On the tables are harbourmasters' registers, log books, treatises on sailing, various nautical periodicals, and several volumes with colour plates which show legendary clippers and ocean-going steamers such as the Conte di Savoia or the Mauretania, giants of iron and steel, more than three hundred yards long, into which the Washington Capitol might have fitted, their funnels so tall they vanished into the low-hanging clouds. The Reading Room in Southwold is opened every morning at seven (save only on Christmas Day) and remains open until almost midnight. At best, it attracts a handful of visitors during the holidays, and the few who do cross the threshold leave again after they have taken a brief look around in the uncomprehending way characteristic of such holidaymakers. The Reading Room is thus almost always deserted but for one or two of the surviving fishermen and seafarers sitting in silence in the armchairs, whiling the hours away. Sometimes, in the evenings, they play a game of pool in the back room. Apart from the muffled sound of the sea and the clicking of the balls there is nothing to be heard then, except perhaps, from time to time, the slight scratching noise made by a player priming his cue and the short puff when he blows off the chalk. Whenever I am in Southwold, the Sailors' Reading Room is by far my favourite haunt. It is better than anywhere else for reading, writing letters, following one's thoughts, or in the long winter months simply looking out at the stormy sea as it crashes on the promenade. So on this occasion too I entered the Reading Room to see whether anything had changed and to make notes on things that had occurred to me during the day. At first, as on some of my earlier visits, I leafed through the log of the Southwold, a patrol ship that was anchored off the pier from autumn of 1914. On the large landscape-format pages, a fresh one for each new date, there are occasional entries surrounded by a good deal of empty space, reading, for instance, Maurice Farman Bi-plane N'ward Inland or White Steam-yacht Flying White Ensign Cruising on Horizon to S. Every time I decipher one of these entries I am astounded that a trail that has long since vanished from the air or the water remains visible here on the paper. That morning, as I closed the marbled cover of the log book, pondering the mysterious survival of the written word, I noticed lying to one side on the table a thick, tattered tome that I had not seen before on my visits to the Reading Room. It turned out to be a photographic history of the First World War, compiled and published in 1933 by the *Daily Express*, to mark the past tragedy, and perhaps as a warning of another approaching. Every theatre of war is documented in this compendious collection, from the Vall' Inferno on the Austro-Italian Alpine front to Flanders fields. There are illustrations of all conceivable forms of violent death, from the shooting down of a single aviation pioneer over the Somme estuary to the mass slaughter in the swamps of Galicia, and pictures of French towns reduced to rubble, corpses rotting in the no-man's-land between the trenches, woodlands razed by artillery fire, battleships sinking under black clouds of petroleum smoke, armies on the march, never-ending streams of refugees, shattered zeppelins, scenes from Prszemysl and St Quentin, from Montfaucon and Gallipoli, scenes of destruction, mutilation, desecration, starvation, conflagration, and freezing cold. The titles are almost without exception bitterly ironic –

When Cities Deck Their Streets for War! This was a Forest! This was a Man! There is some Corner of a Foreign Field that is Forever England! One section of the book is devoted to the chaos in the Balkans, a part of the world which was further removed from England then than Lahore or Omdurman. Page after page of pictures from Serbia, Bosnia and Albania show scattered groups of people and stray individuals trying to escape the War by ox-cart, in the heat of summer, along dusty country roads, or on foot through drifting snow with a pony half-dead with exhaustion. The chronicle of disaster opens with the notorious snapshot from Sarajevo. The picture has the caption Princip Lights the Fuse!

It is the 28th of June 1914, a bright, sunny day, ten forty-five in the morning. One sees a few Bosnians, some Austrian military personnel, and the assassin being apprehended. The facing page shows the tunic of Archduke Franz Ferdinand's uniform, holed by bullets and soaked with blood, which must have been photographed for the press after being stripped from the body of the heir to the throne and transferred by rail to the capital of the empire, where it can be viewed to this day, together with his feather bushed hat and trousers, in a black-framed reliquary in the army museum. Gavrilo Princip was the son of a Grahovo valley farmer, and until recently had been a grammar-school pupil in Belgrade. After being sentenced he was locked up in the Theresienstadt casemates, and there, in April 1918, he died of the bone tuberculosis that had been consuming him since his early youth. In 1993 the Serbs celebrated the seventy-fifth anniversary of his death.

On the following day I sat alone till tea time in the bar restaurant of the Crown Hotel. The rattle of crockery in the kitchen had long since subsided; in the grandfather clock, with its rising and setting sun and a moon that appears at night, the cogwheels gripped, the pendulum swung from side to side, and the big hand, bit by bit, in tiny jerks, went its round. For some time I had been feeling a sense of eternal peace when, leafing through the *Independent on Sunday*, I came across an article that was related to the Balkan pictures I had seen in the Reading Room the previous evening. The article, which was about the so-called cleansing operations carried out fifty years ago in Bosnia, by the Croats together with the Austrians and the Germans, began by describing a photograph taken as a souvenir by men of the Croatian Ustasha, in which fellow militiamen in the best of spirits, some of them striking heroic poses, are sawing off the head of a Serb named Branco Jungic. A second snap shows the severed head with a cigarette between lips still parted in a last cry of pain. This happened at Jasenovac camp on the Sava. Seven hundred thousand men, women and children were killed there alone in ways that made even the hair of the Reich's experts stand on end, as some of them are said to have admitted when they were amongst themselves. The preferred instruments of execution were saws and sabres, axes and hammers, and leather cuff-bands with fixed blades that were fastened on the lower arm and made especially in Solingen for the purpose of cutting throats, as well as a kind of rudimentary cross-bar gallows on which the Serbs, Jews and Bosnians, once rounded

up, were hanged in rows like crows or magpies. Not far from Jasenovac, in a radius of no more than ten miles, there were also the camps of Prijedor, Stara Gradiska and Banja Luka, where the Croatian militia, its hand strengthened by the Wehrmacht and its spirit by the Catholic church, performed one day's work after another in similar manner. The history of this massacre, which went on for years, is recorded in fifty thousand documents abandoned by the Germans and Croats in 1945, which are kept to this day, according to the author of the 1992 article, in the Bosanske Krajine Archive in Banja Luka, which is, or used to be, housed in what was once an Austro-Hungarian barracks, serving in 1942 as the headquarters of the Heeresgruppe E intelligence division. Without a doubt those who were stationed there knew what was going on in the Ustasha camps, just as they knew of the enormities perpetrated during the Kozara campaign against Tito's partisans, for instance, in the course of which between sixty and ninety thousand people were killed in so-called acts of war, that is to say were executed, or died as a result of deportation. The female population of Kozara was transported to Germany and worked to death in the slave-labour system that extended over the entire territory of the Reich. Of the children who were left behind, twenty-three thousand in number, the militia murdered half on the spot, while the rest were herded together at various assembly points to be sent on to Croatia; of these, not a few died of typhoid fever, exhaustion and fear, even before the cattle wagons reached the Croatian capital. Many of those who were still alive were so hungry that they had eaten the cardboard identity tags they wore about their necks and thus in their extreme desperation had eradicated their own names. Later they were brought up as Catholics in Croatian families, and sent to confession and their first holy communion. Like everyone else they learnt the socialist ABC at school, chose an occupation, and became railway workers, salesgirls, tool-fitters or book-keepers. But no one knows what shadowy memories haunt them to this day. In this connection one might also add that one of the Heeresgruppe E intelligence officers at that time was a young Viennese lawyer whose chief task was to draw up memoranda relating to the necessary resettlements, described as imperative for humanitarian reasons. For this commendable paperwork he was awarded by Croatian head of state Ante Pavelić the silver medal of the crown of King Zvonomir, with oak leaves. In the post-war years this officer, who at the very start of his career was so promising and so very competent in the technicalities of administration, occupied various high offices, among them that of Secretary General of the United Nations. And reportedly it was in this last capacity that he spoke onto tape, for the benefit of any extra-terrestrials that may happen to share our universe, words of greeting that are now, together with other memorabilia of mankind, approaching the outer limits of our solar system aboard the space probe Voyager II.

V

On the second evening of my stay in Southwold, after the late news, the BBC broadcast a documentary about Roger Casement, who was executed in a London prison in 1916 for high treason. The images in this film, many of which were taken

from rare archive footage, immediately captivated me; but nonetheless, I fell asleep in the green velvet armchair I had pulled up to the television. As my waking consciousness ebbed away, I could still hear every word of the narrator's account of Casement with singular clarity, but was unable to grasp their meaning. And when

I emerged hours later, from the depths of a dream, to see in the first light of dawn the test card quivering in the silent box, all I could recall was that the programme had begun with an account of Casement's meeting with the writer Joseph Conrad in the Congo. Conrad considered Casement the only man of integrity among the Europeans whom he had encountered there, and who had been corrupted partly by the tropical climate and partly by their own rapaciousness and greed. I've seen him start off into an unspeakable wilderness (thus the exact words of a quotation from Conrad, which has remained in my head) swinging a crookhandled stick, with two bulldogs: Paddy (white) and Biddy (brindle) at his heels and a Loanda boy carrying a bundle. A few months afterwards it so happened that I saw him come out again, leaner, a little browner, with his stick, dogs, and Loanda boy, and quietly serene as though he had been for a stroll in the park. Since I had lost the rest of the narrator's account of the lives of Casement and Conrad, except for these few words and some shadowy images of the two men, I have since tried to reconstruct from the sources, as far as I have been able, the story I slept through that night in Southwold.

In the late summer of 1861, Mme Evelina Korzeniowska travelled from the small Ukrainian town of Zhitomir to Warsaw, with her boy Józef Teodor Konrad, then not quite five, to join her husband Apollo Korzeniowski, who that spring had already given up his unrewarding position as an estate manager with the intention of helping pave the way for a revolt against Russian tyranny through his writings and by means of conspiratorial politics. In mid-October the illegal Polish National Committee met for its first sessions in Korzeniowski's Warsaw flat, and over the next few weeks the young

Konrad doubtless saw many mysterious persons coming and going at his parents' home. The serious expressions of the gentlemen talking in muted tones in the white and red salon will have suggested the significance of that historic hour to him and he may even, at that point, have been initiated into the clandestine proceedings, and have understood that Mama wore black, which was expressly forbidden by law, as a token of mourning for her people suffering the humiliation of foreign rule. If not, he was taken into their confidence at the end of October at the latest, when his father was arrested and imprisoned in the citadel. After a cursory hearing before a military tribunal Apollo Korzeniowski was sentenced to exile in Vologda, a god-forsaken town somewhere in the wastes beyond Nizhni Novgorod. Vologda, he wrote in summer 1863 to his Zagórski cousins, is a great three-verst marsh across which logs and tree trunks are placed parallel to each other in crooked lines; the houses, even the garishly painted wooden palaces of the provincial grandees, are erected on piles driven into the morass at intervals. Everything round about rots, decays and sinks into the ground. There are only two seasons: the white winter and the green winter. For nine months the ice-cold air sweeps down from the Arctic sea. The thermometer plunges to unbelievable depths and one is surrounded by a limitless darkness. During the green winter it rains week in week out. The mud creeps over the threshold, rigor mortis is temporarily lifted and a few signs of life, in the form of an all-pervasive marasmus, begin to manifest themselves. In the white winter everything is dead, during the green winter everything is dying.

The tuberculosis which had ailed Evelina Korzeniowska for years advanced unimpeded in these conditions. The days that remained to her were numbered. When the Czarist authorities granted her a compassionate stay of sentence in order that she might spend a longer spell on her brother's estate in the Ukraine, to recover her health, it was no more than an additional torment; for after the period of reprieve expired she had to return into exile with Konrad, despite all her petitions and applications and despite the fact that she was now more dead than alive. On the day of her departure, Evelina Korzeniowska stood on the steps of the manor house at Nowofastów surrounded by her relations, the servants, and friends from the neighbouring domains. Everyone there assembled, apart from the children and those in livery, is attired in black cloth or black silk. Not a single word is spoken. Grandmother stoically stares out past the sad scene into the deserted countryside. On the sweeping sandy drive that curves around the circular yew hedge a bizarre, elongated carriage is waiting. The shafts protrude much too far forward, and the coachman's box seems a long way from the rear of the strange conveyance, which is overloaded with trunks and chests of every description. The carriage is slung low between the wheels as if between two worlds drifting ever further apart. The carriage door is open, and inside, on the cracked leather seat, young Konrad has been settled for some time, watching from the dark the scene he will later describe. Poor Mama, inconsolable, looks around her for the last time, then descends the steps on the arm of Uncle Tadeusz. Those who remain behind retain their composure. Even Konrad's favourite cousin, who is wearing a short skirt of a tartan pattern and resembles a princess amidst the black-clad gathering, just puts her fingertips to her lips to indicate her horror at the departure of the two banished exiles. And ungainly Mlle Durand from Switzerland, the governess who has devoted herself to Konrad's education all summer with the utmost energy and who would otherwise avail herself of any opportunity to burst into tears, valiantly appeals to her charge as she waves a farewell handkerchief: N'oublie pas ton français, mon chéri! Uncle Tadeusz closes the carriage door and takes a step back. The coach lurches forward. The friends and relatives vanish from Konrad's view through the small window, and when he looks out at the other side he sees, in the distance, halfway down to the great gates, the district police commandant's light, open trap, harnessed to three horses in Russian fashion, drawn up on one side and the commandant himself sitting in it, the vizor of his flat cap with its red band pulled down over his eyes.

In early April 1865, eighteen months after the departure from Nowofastów, Evelina Korzeniowska died in exile aged thirty-two of the shadows that her tuberculosis had spread through her body, and of the home-sickness that was corroding her soul. Apollo's will to live was also almost extinguished. He was quite unable now to devote himself to his troubled son's education, and hardly ever pursued his own work at all. The most he could do was to alter the odd line or two in his translation of Victor Hugo's *Les travailleurs de la mer*. That prodigiously boring book seemed to him to mirror his own life. C'est un livre sur des destinées dépaysées, he once said to Konrad, sur des individus expulsés et perdus, sur les éliminés du sort, un livre sur ceux qui sont seuls et évités. In 1867, a few days before Christmas, Apollo Korzeniowski was released from his Russian exile. The authorities had decided that he no longer constituted a threat, and gave him a passport valid for one journey to Madeira, for purposes of convalescence.

But neither Apollo's financial position nor his frail state of health allowed him to travel. After a short stay in Lemberg, which he found too Austrian for his liking, he rented a few rooms in Poselska Street in Cracow. There he spent most of the time in his armchair, grieving for his lost wife, for the wasted years, and for his poor and lonely boy, who had just written a patriotic play entitled *The Eyes of Johan Sobieski.* Apollo had burnt all of his own manuscripts in the fireplace. At times, when he did so, a weightless flake of soot ash like a scrap of black silk would drift through the room, borne up on the air, before sinking to the floor somewhere or dissolving into the dark. For Apollo, as for Evelina, the end came in the spring, as it was beginning to thaw, but it was not granted to him to depart this life on the anniversary of her death. He lay in his bed till well into May, becoming steadily weaker and thinner. During those weeks when his father was dying, Konrad would sit at a little table lit by a green lamp in a windowless cabinet to do his homework in the late afternoon after school. The ink stains in his exercise book and on his hands came from the fear in his heart. Whenever the door of the next room opened he could hear his father's shallow breathing. Two nuns with snow-white wimples were tending the patient. Without a sound they glided hither and thither, performing their duties and occasionally casting a concerned glance at the child who would soon be orphaned, bent over his writing, adding up numbers or reading, hour after hour, voluminous Polish and French adventure stories, novels and travel books.

The funeral of the patriot Apollo Korzeniowski was a great demonstration, conducted in silence. Along the streets, which were closed to traffic, bare-headed workmen, schoolchildren, university students and citizens, who had doffed their top hats, stood in solemn emotion, and at every open upper-storey window there were clusters of people dressed in black. The cortège, led by eleven-year-old Konrad as chief mourner, moved out of the narrow side street, through the centre of the town, past the Church of Mary the Virgin with its two unequal towers, towards Florian's Gate. It was a fine afternoon. The blue sky compassed the rooftops and on high the clouds scudded before the wind like a squadron of sailboats. During the funeral, as the priest in his heavy silver-embroidered vestments was intoning the ritual words for the dead man in the pit, Konrad perhaps raised his eyes and beheld the clouds drifting by, seeing them as he had never done before, and perhaps it was then that the thought occurred to him of becoming a sea captain, an altogether unheard-of notion for the son of a Polish gentleman. Three years later he expressed this wish to his guardian for the first time, and nothing on earth could put it out of his mind thereafter, not even when Uncle Tadeusz sent him to Switzerland for a summer holiday of several weeks with his private tutor, Pulman. The tutor was under instructions to remind his charge at every opportunity of the many careers that were open to him beside seafaring, but no matter what he said (at the Rhine falls near Schaffhausen, in Hospenthal, viewing the St Gotthard tunnel under construction, or up on the Furka Pass), Konrad stuck tenaciously to his resolve. Scarcely a year later, on the 14th of October 1874, when he was not yet seventeen, he took leave of his grandmother Teofila Bobrowska and his good Uncle Tadeusz, as they stood on the platform at Cracow outside the train window. The ticket to Marseilles in his pocket had cost one hundred and thirty-seven guilders and seventy-five groschen. He took with him no more than would fit into his small case, and it would be almost sixteen years before he returned to visit his native country again.

In 1875 Konrad Korzeniowski crossed the Atlantic for the first time, on the barque Mont Blanc. At the end of July he was on Martinique, where the ship lay at anchor for two months. The homeward voyage took almost a quarter of a year. It was not until Christmas Day that the Mont Blanc, badly damaged by winter storms, made Le Havre. Undeterred by this tough initiation into life at sea, Konrad Korzeniowski signed on for further voyages to the West Indies, where he visited Cap-Haïtien, Port-au-Prince, St Thomas and St Pierre, which was devastated soon afterwards when Mount Pelée erupted.

On the outward sailing the ship carried arms, steam-powered engines, gunpowder and ammunition. On the return the cargo was sugar and timber. He spent the time when he was not at sea in Marseilles, among fellow sailors and also with people of greater refinement. At the Café Boudol in the rue Saint-Ferréol and in the salon of Mme Déléstang, whose husband was a banker and ship owner, he frequented gatherings that included aristocrats, bohemians, financiers, adventurers, and Spanish Legitimists. The dying throes of courtly life went side by side with the most unscrupulous machinations, complex intrigues were connived at, smuggling syndicates were founded, and shady deals agreed. Korzeniowski was involved in many things, spent more than he had, and succumbed to the advances of a mysterious lady who, though just his own age, was already a widow. This lady, whose true identity has not been established with any certainty, was known as Rita in Legitimist circles, where she played a prominent part; and it was said that she had been the mistress of Don Carlos, the Bourbon prince, whom there were plans to instate, by hook or by crook, on the Spanish throne. Subsequently it was rumoured in various quarters that Doña Rita, who resided in a villa in rue Sylvabelle, and one Paula de Somogyi were one and the same person. The story went that in November 1877, when Don Carlos returned to Vienna from inspecting the front line in the Russo-Turkish war, he asked a certain Mme Hannover to procure for him a Pest chorus girl by the name of Paula Horváth, whose beauty had caught his eye. From Vienna, with his new companion, Don Carlos travelled first to see his brother in Graz and then onward to Venice, Modena and Milan, where he introduced her in society as the Baroness de Somogyi. The rumour that the two mistresses were in reality one person originated in the fact that Rita vanished from Marseilles at the exact moment in time when the Baroness, supposedly because Don Carlos was having a crisis of conscience prompted by the imminent first holy communion of his son Jaime, was either dropped by the Don or married off to the tenor Angel de Trabadelo, with whom she appears to have lived in London in happiness and contentment until her death in 1917. While the matter of whether Rita and Paula were identical must remain unresolved, it is beyond doubt that the young Korzeniowski sought to win the favour of either the one or the other lady, irrespective of whether she had grown up as a goatherd in the highlands of Catalonia or as a goosegirl on the shores of Lake Balaton; just as there is no question that this love story, which in some respects bordered on the fantastic, reached its climax in late February 1877, when Korzeniowski shot himself in the chest, or was shot by a rival. To this day it is unclear whether this wound, which mercifully posed no threat to Korzeniowski's life, was inflicted in a duel, as he himself later claimed, or, as Uncle Tadeusz suspected, in a suicide attempt. Either way, the dramatic gesture, which the young man, who saw himself as a Stendhalien, evidently meant to cut the Gordian knot, took its inspiration from the opera, which at that time determined the social mores and in particular the expressions of love and longing, in Marseilles as in most other European cities. Korzeniowski had seen and heard the work of Rossini and Meyerbeer at the Théatre de Marseille and, above all, was enraptured by the operettas of Jacques Offenbach, which were as much in vogue as ever. A libretto entitled *Konrad Korzeniowski and the*

Carlist Conspiracy in Marseilles could easily have been the making of another of them. In actual fact, however, Korzeniowski's French apprentice years came to an end when he left Marseilles for Constantinople aboard the SS Mavis on the 24th of April 1878. The Russo-Turkish war was over, but from the ship, as he later reported, Korzeniowski was still able to see the army camp at San Stefano, a vast city of white tents, where the peace treaty had been signed, passing by like a mirage. From Constantinople the steamer proceeded to Yeysk, at the far end of the Sea of Asov, where it took on a consignment of linseed oil with which, as the Lowestoft harbour register records, it reached the east coast of England on the 18th of June 1878.

From July until early September, when he left for London, Korzeniowski made three round trips as an ordinary seaman aboard the Skimmer of the Seas, a coaster that plied between Lowestoft and Newcastle. Little is known of how he spent the second half of June in the fishing port and bathing resort of Lowestoft, which could not have afforded a greater contrast to Marseilles. Doubtless he rented a room and made whatever enquiries were necessary for his plans. In the evenings, when the darkness settled upon the sea, he will have strolled along the esplanade, a twenty-one-year-old foreigner alone amongst the English. I can see him, for instance, standing out on the pier, where a brass band is playing the overture from *Tannhäuser* as a night-time serenade. And as he walks homeward past those who remain to listen, with a gentle breeze coming off the water, he is intrigued by the ease with which he is absorbing a hitherto quite unfamiliar language, a language he will one day employ to write the novels that will win him worldwide acclaim, whilst for now it fills him with an altogether new sense of purpose and confidence. By his own account, Korzeniowski's first English tutors were the *Lowestoft Standard* and the *Lowestoft Journal*, in which, during the week of his arrival, the following motley assortment of news items was brought to the public's attention: an explosion in a mine in Wigan cost two hundred lives; in Rumelia there was a Mohammedan uprising; in South Africa the kaffir unrest had to be suppressed; Lord Grenville expatiated on the education of the fair sex; a despatch boat was sent to Marseilles to take the Duke of Cambridge to Malta, where he was to inspect the Indian troops; a housemaid in Whitby was burnt alive when her dress, onto which she had accidentally spilt paraffin, caught light at an open fire; the steamship Largo Bay left the Clyde with three hundred and fifty-two Scottish emigrants aboard; a Mrs Dixon of Silsden was so overjoyed to see her son Thomas, who, after ten years' absence in America, suddenly turned up at her door, that she had a stroke; the young Queen of Spain was growing weaker by the day; work on the fortifications of Hong Kong, where two thousand coolies were slaving, was approaching completion; and in Bosnia, so the *Standard* reports, all highways are infested with bands of robbers, some of them mounted. Even the forests around Sarajevo are swarming with marauders, deserters and francs-tireurs of all kinds. Travelling, therefore, is at a standstill.

In February 1890, twelve years after his arrival in Lowestoft and fifteen years after his departure from the station at Cracow, Korzeniowski, who now had British citizenship and his captain's papers and had seen the most far-flung regions of the earth, returned for the first time to Kazimierówka and the house of his Uncle Tadeusz. In a note written much later he described his arrival at the Ukrainian station after brief stops in Berlin, Warsaw and Lublin. There his uncle's coachman and majordomo were waiting for him in a sleigh to which four duns were harnessed but which was so small that it almost looked like a toy. The ride to Kazimierówka took another eight hours. The majordomo wrapped me up solicitously, writes Korzeniowski, in a bearskin coat that reached to the tips of my toes and put an enormous fur hat with ear flaps on my head, before taking his seat beside me. When the sleigh started off, to a soft and even jingle of bells, a winter journey back into childhood began for me. The young coachman, who was perhaps only sixteen years old, found the way across the endless snow-covered fields with an unfailing instinct. When I commented on his astounding sense of direction (Korzeniowski continues), never hesitating and not once taking a wrong turn, the majordomo replied that the young fellow was the son of Joseph, who had always driven grandmother Bobrowska of blessed memory and later served Pan Tadeusz with equal loyalty, until cholera ended his days. His wife, the majordomo said, died of the cholera too, which reached us when the ice was breaking, and so did a whole houseful of children, and the only one who survived was this deaf mute sitting in front of us on the box. He was never sent to school and no one ever expected he would be much use for anything till it turned out that horses were more obedient to him than to any other stable-boy. And when he was about eleven it emerged on some occasion or other that he had the map of the entire district in his head, complete with every bend in the road, so accurately you'd think he'd been born with it. Never, writes Korzeniowski, have I travelled better than that day as we journeyed into the settling dusk. As in the old days, long ago, I saw the sun going down over the plains, a great red disc sinking into the snow as though it were setting upon the sea. Swiftly we drove on into the gathering dark, into the infinite white wastes that met the starry skies at the horizon, where villages amidst trees floated like shadowy islands.

Before he set off for Poland and the Ukraine, Korzeniowski had applied for a job with the Société Anonyme Belge pour le Commerce du Haut-Congo. Immediately after his return to Brussels he called in person on the managing director, Albert Thys, at the Société's main offices in Brederodestraat. Thys, whose shapeless body was forced into a frock coat that was far too tight, was sitting in a gloomy office beneath a map of Africa that covered the entire wall, and the moment Korzeniowski had stated his business, without further ado, he offered him the command of a steamer that plied the upper reaches of the Congo, because the captain, a German or Dane by the name of Freiesleben, had, as it happened, just been killed by the natives. After two weeks of hasty preparation and a cursory medical, conducted by the Société's ghoulish doctor, Korzeniowski took the train to Bordeaux, where in mid-May he embarked on the Ville de Maceió, bound for Boma. At Tenerife he was already beset with dark premonitions. Life, he wrote to his beautiful and recently widowed Aunt Marguerite Poradowska in Brussels, is a tragicomedy – beaucoup de rêves, un rare éclair de bonheur, un peu de colère, puis la désillusion, des années de souffrance et la fin – in which, for better or worse, one had to play one's part. In the course of the long voyage, in this dispirited frame of mind, the madness of the whole colonial enterprise was gradually borne in upon Korzeniowski. Day after day the coastline was unchanging, as if the vessel were making no progress. And yet, wrote Korzeniowski, we passed a number of landing places and trading posts with names like Gran' Bassam or Little Popo, all of them seeming to belong in some sordid farce. Once we passed a warship anchored off a dreary beach where not the smallest sign of any settlement was to be seen. As far as the eye could reach there was nothing but ocean, sky, and the hair-thin green strip of bush vegetation. The ensign hung limp from the mast, the ponderous iron vessel rose and fell on the slimy swell, and at regular intervals the long six-inch guns fired off shells into the unknown African continent, with neither purpose nor aim.

Bordeaux, Tenerife, Dakar, Conakry, Sierra Leone, Cotonou, Libreville, Loango, Banane, Boma – after four weeks at sea, Korzeniowski at last reached the Congo, one of those remote destinations he had dreamt of as a child. At that time the Congo had been but a white patch on the map of Africa over which he had often pored for hours, reciting the colourful names. Little was marked in the interior of this part of the world, no railway lines, no roads, no towns, and, as cartographers would often embellish such empty spaces with drawings of exotic beasts, a roaring lion or a crocodile with gaping jaws, they had rendered the Congo, of which they knew only that it was a river measuring thousands of miles from its source to the sea, as a snake coiling through the blank, uncharted land. Since then, of course, detail had been added to the map. The white patch had become a place of darkness. And the fact is that in the entire history of colonialism, most of it not yet written, there is scarcely a darker chapter than the one termed *The Opening of the Congo*. When the Association Internationale pour l'Exploration et la Civilisation en Afrique was established in September 1876, it was with a declaration of the most high-minded intentions and ostensibly without any vested national or private interests. Exalted personages representing the aristocracy, the churches, the sciences, industry and finance, attended the inaugural meeting, at which King Leopold, patron of the exemplary venture, proclaimed that the friends of humanity could pursue no nobler end than that which brought them together that day: to open up the last part of our earth to have remained hitherto untouched by the blessings of civilization. The aim, said King Leopold, was to break through the darkness in which whole peoples still dwelt, and to mount a crusade in order to bring this glorious century of progress to the point of perfection. In the nature of things, the lofty spirit expressed in this declaration was later lost from sight. As early as 1885, Leopold, now styled Souverain de l'État Independant du Congo, was the sole ruler of a territory on the second longest river on earth, a million square miles in area and thus a hundred times the size of the mother country, and was accountable to no one for his actions. Ruthlessly he set about exploiting its inexhaustible wealth, through trading companies such as the Société Anonyme Belge pour le Commerce du Haut-Congo, the soon legendary profits of which were built on a system of slave labour which was sanctioned by all the shareholders and all the Europeans contracted to work in the new colony. In some parts of the Congo, the indigenous people were all but eradicated by forced labour, and those who were taken there from other parts of Africa or from overseas died in droves of dysentery, malaria, smallpox, beriberi, jaundice, starvation, and physical exhaustion. Every year from 1890 to 1900, an estimated five hundred thousand of these nameless victims, nowhere mentioned in the annual reports, lost their lives. During the same period, the value of shares in the Compagnie du Chemin de Fer du Congo rose from 320 Belgian francs to 2,850.

On arrival in Boma, Korzeniowski transferred from the Ville de Maceió to a small river steamer, by which he reached Matadi on the 13th of June. From there he went overland, since numerous waterfalls and rapids make the Congo unnavigable from Matadi to Stanley Pool. Matadi was a desolate settlement, known to its inhabitants as the town of stones. Like an ulcer it festered on the rubble thrown up over thousands of years by the infernal cauldron at the end of this three hundred-mile stretch of the river, which remains untamed even today. Buildings with rusty corrugated iron roofs were dotted randomly below the high crags through which the water forced its way, and amongst these, on the scree, and on the steep riverbank slopes, gangs of black figures were everywhere at work or moving in bearer columns that ran long lines across the rough terrain. Here and there an overseer in white suit and white pith helmet stood by. Korzeniowski had already been for a day or so in this arena reminiscent of a quarry, where the constant noise of the rapids filled the air, when (as Marlow later describes in *Heart of Darkness*) he came upon a place some way off from the settlement where those who were racked by illness, starvation and toil had withdrawn to die. As if after a massacre they lay there in the greenish gloom at the bottom of the gorge. Evidently no one cared to stop these black shadows when they crept off into the bush. I began to distinguish the gleam of the eyes under the trees, says Marlow. Then, glancing down, I saw a face near my hand. The black bones reclined at full length with one shoulder against the tree, and slowly the eyelids rose and the sunken eyes looked up at me, enormous and vacant, a kind of blind, white flicker in the depths of the orbs, which died out slowly. And as this man, scarcely more than a boy, breathed his last, those who were not yet worn out were carrying hundred-weight sacks of provisions, crates of tools, explosive charges, gear and equipment of every description, engines, spare parts, and sections of ships' hulls through the swamps and forests and across the sun-scorched uplands, or were working in the mountain range of Palaballa and by the M'Pozo river, building a railway to link Matadi with the upper reaches of the Congo. Korzeniowski made that arduous journey himself, along a route where presently the settlements of Songolo, Thumba and Thysville would be established. He had with him a caravan of thirty-one men and, as his troublesome travelling companion, an overweight Frenchman named Harou, who invariably fainted whenever they were miles from the nearest shade, so that for long distances he had to be transported in a hammock. The march took well-nigh forty days, and during this period Korzeniowski began to grasp that his own travails did not absolve him from the guilt which he had incurred by his mere presence in the Congo. Though he did in fact continue upriver from Léopoldville, aboard the steamer Roi des

Belges, to the Stanley Falls, he now regarded his original plan of taking up a command for the Société Anonyme with revulsion. The corrosive humidity of the air, the sunlight pulsing to the heartbeat, the unchanging haze that hung over the river, and the company he had to keep aboard the Roi des Belges, which struck him increasingly, as the days went by, as unhinged – he knew that he would have to turn back. Tout m'est antipathique ici, he wrote to Marguerite Poradowska, les hommes et les choses, mais surtout les hommes. Tous ces boutiquiers africains et marchands d'ivoire aux instincts sordides. Je regrette d'être venu ici. Je le regrette même amèrement. Back in Léopoldville, Korzeniowski was so sick in body and in soul that he longed for death. But it was to be another three months before this man, whose protracted bouts of despair were henceforth to alternate with his writing, was able to depart homeward from Boma. In mid-January 1891 he reached Ostend, the selfsame port that one Joseph Loewy left some days later aboard the steamship Belgian Prince, bound for Boma. Loewy, an uncle of Franz Kafka, who was then seven years old, was a Panama veteran and thus knew what was in store for him. Ahead lay a total of twelve years (including five sojourns in Europe of several months in spa towns and mountain resorts), during which time he held various important positions in Matadi, where life for people such as himself gradually became more tolerable. In July 1896, for instance, at a banquet to mark the opening of the halfway station at Thumba, not only local delicacies but also European foods and wines were served to the guests. Two years after that memorable occasion, Loewy (at far left in the photograph),

now director of the entire trading division, was awarded the Gold Medal of the Ordre du Lion Royal by King Leopold himself, at a ceremony to mark the completion of the Congo railway. Korzeniowski, who travelled onward to see Marguerite Poradowska in Brussels immediately after arriving in Ostend, now saw the capital of the Kingdom of Belgium, with its ever more bombastic buildings, as a sepulchral monument erected over a hecatomb of black bodies, and all the passers-by in the streets seemed to him to bear that dark Congolese secret within them. And indeed, to this day one sees in Belgium a distinctive ugliness, dating from the time when the Congo colony was exploited without restraint and manifested in the macabre atmosphere of certain salons and the strikingly stunted growth of the population, such as one rarely comes across elsewhere. At all events, I well recall that on my first visit to Brussels in December 1964

I encountered more hunchbacks and lunatics than normally in a whole year. One evening in a bar in Rhode St Genèse I even watched a deformed billiard player who was racked with spastic contortions but who was able, when it was his turn and he had taken a moment to steady himself, to play the most difficult cannons with unerring precision. The hotel by the Bois de la Cambre where I was then lodging for a few days was so crammed with heavy mahogany furniture, all manner of African trophies, and pot plants, some of which were quite enormous, among them aspidistras, monsterae and rubber plants reaching almost to the twelve-feet-high ceiling, that even in broad daylight the interior seemed darkened with chocolate-coloured gloom. I still see quite clearly the massive, elaborately carved sideboard, on one side of which stood a glass case containing an arrangement of artificial twigs, colourful silk bows and tiny stuffed humming-birds, and on the other a conical pile of china fruit. But ever since that first visit to Brussels, the very definition of Belgian ugliness, in my eyes, has been the Lion Monument and the so-called historical memorial site of the Battle of Waterloo.

Why I went to Waterloo I no longer know. But I do remember walking from the bus stop past a bleak field and a number of ramshackle buildings to a sort of village, which consisted solely of souvenir shops and cheap restaurants. There were no visitors about on that leaden-grey day shortly before Christmas, not even the obligatory group of schoolchildren one inevitably encounters in such a place. But as if they had come to people this deserted stage, a squad of characters in Napoleonic costume suddenly appeared tramping up and down the few streets, beating drums and blowing fifes; and bringing up the rear was a slatternly, garishly made-up sutler woman pulling a curious handcart with a goose shut in a cage. For a while I watched these mummers, who seemed to be in perpetual motion, as they disappeared amongst the buildings only to re-emerge elsewhere. At length I bought a ticket for the Waterloo Panorama, housed in an immense domed rotunda, where from a raised platform in the middle one can view the battle – a favourite subject with panorama artists – in every direction. It is like being at the centre of events. On a sort of landscaped proscenium, immediately below the wooden rail amidst tree-stumps and undergrowth in the blood-stained sand, lie lifesize horses, and cut-down infantrymen, hussars and chevaux-légers, eyes rolling in pain or already extinguished. Their faces are moulded from wax but the boots, the leather belts, the weapons, the cuirasses, and the splendidly coloured uniforms, probably stuffed with eelgrass, rags and the like, are to all appearances authentic. Across this horrific three-dimensional scene, on which the cold dust of time has settled, one's gaze is drawn to the horizon, to the enormous mural, one hundred and ten yards by twelve, painted in 1912 by the French marine artist Louis Dumontin on the inner wall of the circus-like structure. This then, I thought, as I looked round about me, is the representation of history. It requires a falsification of perspective. We, the survivors, see everything from above, see everything at once, and still we do not know how it was. The desolate field extends all around where once fifty thousand soldiers and ten thousand horses met their end within a few hours. The night after the battle, the air must have been filled with death rattles and groans. Now there is nothing but the silent brown soil. Whatever became of the corpses and mortal remains? Are they buried under the memorial? Are we standing on a mountain of death? Is that our ultimate vantage point? Does one really have the much-vaunted historical overview from such a position? Near Brighton, I was once told, not far from the coast, there are two copses that were planted after the Battle of Waterloo in remembrance of that memorable victory. One is in the shape of a Napoleonic three-cornered hat, the other in that of a Wellington boot. Naturally the outlines cannot be made out from the ground; they were intended as landmarks for latter-day balloonists. That afternoon in the rotunda I inserted a couple of coins in a slot machine to hear an account of the battle in Flemish. Of the various circumstances and vicissitudes described I understood no more than the odd phrase. De holle weg van Ohain, de Hertog van Wellington, de rook van de pruisische batterijen, tegenaanval van de nederlandse cavalerie – the fighting will have surged to and fro in waves for a long time, as is generally the case.

No clear picture emerged. Neither then nor today. Only when I had shut my eyes, I well recall, did I see a cannonball smash through a row of poplars at an angle, sending the green branches flying in tatters. And then I saw Fabrizio, Stendhal's young hero, wandering about the battlefield, pale but with his eyes aglow, and an unsaddled colonel getting to his feet and telling his sergeant: I can feel nothing but the old injury in my right hand. – Before returning to Brussels I warmed up a little in one of the restaurants. At the far end of the room, in the dim light that entered by the Belgian bulls'-eye panes, sat a hunchbacked pensioner. She was wearing a woollen cap, a winter coat made of thick burled material, and fingerless gloves. The waitress brought her a plate with a huge piece of meat. The old woman stared at it for a while, then produced from her handbag a small, sharp knife with a wooden handle and began to cut it up. She would have been born, it occurs to me now, at about the time that the Congo railway was completed.

The first news of the nature and extent of the crimes committed against the native peoples in the course of opening up the Congo came to public attention in 1903 through Roger Casement, then British consul at Boma. In a memorandum to Foreign Secretary Lord Lansdowne, Casement – who, so Korzeniowski told a London acquaintance, could tell things that he, Korzeniowski, had long been trying to forget – gave an exact account of the utterly merciless exploitation of the blacks. They were compelled to work unpaid throughout the colony, given a bare minimum to eat, often in chain-gangs, and labouring to a set timetable from dawn to dusk till in the end they literally dropped dead. Anyone who travelled the upper reaches of the Congo and was not blinded by greed for money, wrote Casement, would behold the agony of an entire race in all its heart-rending details, a suffering that eclipsed even the most calamitous tales in the Bible. Casement made it perfectly clear that hundreds of thousands of slave labourers were being worked to death every year by their white overseers, and that mutilation, by severing hands and feet, and execution by revolver, were among the everyday punitive means of maintaining discipline in the Congo. King Leopold invited Casement to Brussels for a personal talk aimed either at defusing the tension created by Casement's intervention or at assessing the threat his activities posed to the Belgian colonial enterprise. Leopold explained that he considered the work done by the blacks as a perfectly legitimate alternative to the payment of taxes, and if the white supervisory personnel at times went too far, as he did not deny, it was due to the fact that the climate of the Congo triggered a kind of dementia in the brains of some whites, which unfortunately it was not always possible to prevent in time, a fact which was regrettable but could hardly be changed. Since Casement's views could not be altered with arguments of this kind, Leopold availed himself of his royal privilege in London, as a result of which, with a certain duplicity, Casement was on the one hand praised for his exemplary report and awarded the CMG, while on the other hand nothing was done that might have had an adverse effect on Belgian interests. When Casement was transferred to South America some years later, probably with the ulterior motive of getting his troublesome person out of the way for a while, he exposed conditions in the jungle areas of Peru, Colombia and Brazil that resembled those in the Congo in many respects, with the difference that here the controlling agent was not Belgian trading associations but the Amazon Company, the head office of which was in the city of London. In South America too, whole tribes were being wiped out at that time and entire regions burnt to the ground. Casement's report, and his unconditional partisanship for the victims and those who had no rights, undoubtedly earned him a certain respect at the Foreign Office, but at the same time many of the top-ranking officials shook their heads at what seemed to them a quixotic zeal incompatible with the professional advancement of otherwise so promising an envoy. They tried to deal with the matter by knighting Casement, in express recognition of his services to the oppressed peoples of the earth. But Casement was not prepared to switch to the side of the powerful; quite the contrary, he was increasingly preoccupied with the nature and origins of that power and the imperialist mentality that resulted from it. It was only to be expected that in due course he should hit upon the Irish question – that is to say, his own. Casement had grown up in County Antrim, the son of a Protestant father and a Catholic mother, and by education and upbringing he was predestined to be one of those whose mission in life was the upholding English rule in Ireland. In the years leading up to the First World War, when the Irish question was becoming acute, Casement espoused the cause of "the white Indians of Ireland". The injustice which had been borne by the Irish for centuries increasingly filled his consciousness. He could not rid his thoughts of the fact that almost half the population of Ireland had been murdered by Cromwell's soldiers, that thousands of men and women were later sent as white slaves to the West Indies, that in recent times more than a million Irish had died of starvation, and that the majority of the young generation were still forced to emigrate from their native land. The moment of decision for Casement came in 1914 when the Home Rule programme proposed by the Liberal government to solve the Irish problem was defeated by the fanatical resistance of Ulster Protestants with the support, both open and covert, of various English interest groups. We will not shrink from Ulster's resistance to Home Rule for Ireland, even if the British Commonwealth is convulsed declared Frederick Smith, one of the leading representatives of the Protestant minority whose so-called loyalism consisted in their willingness to defend their privileges against government troops by force of arms if necessary. The hundred-thousand-strong Ulster Volunteers were founded. In the south, too, an army of volunteers was raised. Casement took part in the recruiting drive and helped equip the contingents. He returned his decorations to London, and refused the pension he had been offered. In early 1915 he travelled to Berlin on a secret mission, to urge the government of the German Reich to supply arms to the Irish army of liberation and persuade Irish prisoners of war in Germany to form an Irish brigade. In both endeavours Casement was unsuccessful, and he was returned to Ireland by a German submarine. Deadly tired and chilled to the bone by the icy water, he waded ashore in the bay of Banna Strand near Tralee. He was now fifty-one; his arrest was imminent.

All he could do was to send the message *No German help available* through a priest, to stop the Easter rising which was planned for all Ireland and was now condemned to failure. If the idealists, poets, trade unionists and teachers who bore the responsibility in Dublin nonetheless sacrificed themselves and those who obeyed them in seven days of street fighting, that was none of his doing. When the rising was put down, Casement was already in a cell in the Tower of London. He had no legal adviser. Counsel for the prosecution was Frederick Smith, who had risen to become Director of Public Prosecutions, which meant that the outcome of the trial was as good as decided before it began. In order to pre-empt any petitions for pardon that might have been made by persons of influence, excerpts from what was known as the Black Diary, a kind of chronicle of the accused's homosexual relations found when Casement's home was searched, were forwarded to the King of England, the President of the United States, and the Pope. The authenticity of this Black Diary, kept until recently under lock and key at the Public Records Office in Kew, was long considered highly debatable, not least because the executive and judicial organs of the state concerned with furnishing the evidence and drawing up the charge against alleged Irish terrorists have repeatedly been guilty, until very recent times, not only of pursuing doubtful suspicions and insinuations but indeed of deliberate falsification of the facts. For the veterans of the Irish freedom movement it was in any case inconceivable that one of their martyrs should have practised the English vice. But since the release to general scrutiny of the diaries in early 1994 there has no longer been any question that they are in

17 51 Lauro of | Manuel Violetta 9

March 29 Sunday—5 in Lent [88–277] 3rd Mo **1903**

Santa Cruz | gone to Las Palmas

● 1h 26m A.M. (Greenwich)

Pepe & Juan again – Stayed in Cabin. Feeling very seedy. Bleeding badly aft again Santa Cruz. Ran 372 miles from S/Leone 393. Will not get in until about 7 pm Tomorrow – so I will probably be kept all night there. I rather hope so – & it will give more time make enquiry for basket. Hope to find it or hear of it. Feeling very seedy indeed. Turned in 10.30 after talk with Bly

30 MONDAY [89–276]
Mohammedan Year 1321 begins

Much hotter today. Busy writing in Cabin in morning. Wrote many letters. Borrowed £20 from Skip for G.B. Ran 327 miles – S/Leone 66 off. arr. there about 6.15. "Teneriffe" in – no sign of basket. Wrote G.B. with £15 to go by "Jebba" tomorrow & other letters about basket.

On shore to agents with Captain Left at 8.35 pm.

Pepe of Guimar 48 52
at Teneriffe 17.

1903 31 TUESDAY [90-275] March & April

Ran 201 miles to noon. Splendid.
288 left to Cape Palmas & total from S/Leone to Axim 840. Read Loti's "Mon frère Yves". Bboy - on board. Read "Smart Set". Very Hot indeed.

"Mon frère Yves" is peculiar

"John" not very well poor old soul with the heat.

1 April WEDNESDAY [91-274]

Very hot
Only did 286 - 2 mile short of Cape Palmas.
Passed along near it - a steamer there. 344 to Axim. Passed Cavally & Tabu & then to sea.
Read 'Les Carnets du Roi'
Stupid Exposition of a Beast - King.

Casement's own hand. We may draw from this the conclusion that it was precisely Casement's homosexuality that sensitized him to the continuing oppression, exploitation, enslavement and destruction, across the borders of social class and race, of those who were furthest from the centres of power. As expected, Casement was found guilty of high treason at the end of his trial at the Old Bailey. The presiding judge, Lord Reading, formerly Rufus Isaacs, pronounced sentence. You will be taken hence, he told Casement, to a lawful prison and thence to a place of execution and will be there hanged by the neck until you be dead. Not until 1965 did the British government permit the exhumation of the remains of Roger Casement, presumably scarcely identifiable any more, from the lime pit in the courtyard of Pentonville prison into which his body had been thrown.

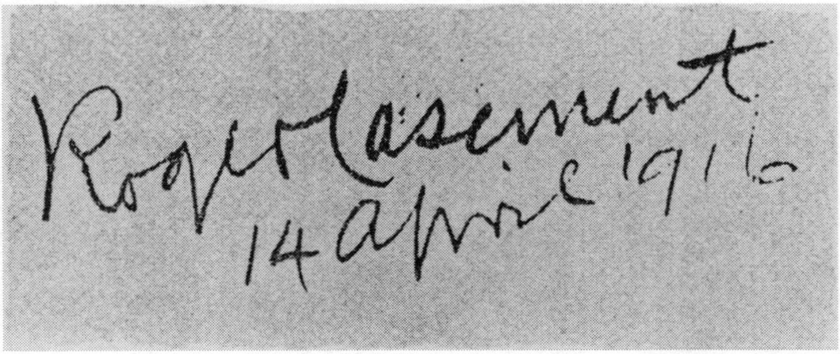

VI

Not far from the coast, between Southwold and Walberswick, a narrow iron bridge crosses the river Blyth where a long

time ago ships heavily laden with wool made their way seaward. Today there is next to no traffic on the river, which is largely silted up. At best one might see a sailing boat or two moored in the lower reaches amidst an assortment of rotting barges. To landward, there is nothing but grey water, mudflats and emptiness.

The bridge over the Blyth was built in 1875 for a narrow-gauge railway that linked Halesworth and Southwold. According to local historians, the train that ran on it had originally been built for the Emperor of China. Precisely which emperor had given this commission I have not succeeded in finding out, despite lengthy research; nor have I been able to discover why the order was never delivered or why this diminutive imperial train, which may have been intended to connect the Palace in Peking, then still surrounded by pinewoods, to one of the summer residences, ended up in service on a branch line of the Great Eastern Railway. The only thing the uncertain sources agree on is that the outlines of the imperial heraldic dragon, complete with a tail and somewhat clouded over by its own breath, could clearly be made out beneath the black paintwork of the carriages, which were used mainly by seaside holidaymakers and travelled at a maximum speed of sixteen miles per hour. As for the heraldic creature itself, the *Libro de los seres imaginarios*, to which reference has already been made, contains a fairly complete taxonomy and description of oriental dragons, of those that inhabit the skies and of those that dwell on the earth and in the seas. Some are said to carry the palaces of the gods on their backs, while others are believed to determine the course of streams and rivers and to guard subterranean treasures. They are armour-plated with yellow scales. Below their muzzles they have beards, their brows beetle over their blazing eyes, their ears are short and fleshy, their mouths invariably hang open, and they feed on pearls and opals. Some are three or four miles long. Mountains crumble when they turn over in their sleep, and when they fly through the air, they cause terrible storms that strip the roofs off houses and devastate the crops. When they rise from the depths of the sea, maelstroms and typhoons ensue. In China, the placating of the elements has always been intimately connected with the ceremonial rites which surrounded the ruler on the dragon throne and which governed everything from affairs of state down to daily ablutions, rituals that also served to legitimize and immortalize the immense profane power that was focused in the person of the emperor. At any moment of the day or night, the members of the imperial household, which numbered more than six thousand and consisted exclusively of eunuchs and women, would be circling, on precisely defined orbits, the sole male inhabitant of the Forbidden City that lay concealed behind purple-coloured walls. In the latter half of the nineteenth century, the ritualization of imperial power was at its most elaborate: at the same time, that power itself was by now almost completely hollowed out. While all court appointments, rigidly controlled as they were by an immutable hierarchy, continued to be made according to rules that had been perfected down to the last detail, the empire in its entirety was on the brink of collapse, owing to mounting pressure from enemies both within and without. In the 1850s and 1860s, the Taiping rebellion, launched by a messianic Christian-Confucian movement, spread like wildfire across all of southern China. Reeling with privation and poverty, the people – from starving peasants and soldiers at large after the Opium war to coolies, sailors, actors and prostitutes – flocked in undreamt-of numbers to the self-appointed Celestial King, Hung Hsiu-ch'üan, who in a feverish delirium had beheld a glorious future in which justice prevailed. Soon a steadily growing army of holy warriors was making its way northwards from Kwangsi. It overran the provinces of Hunan, Hupeh and Anhwei, and in early 1853 was at the gates of the mighty city of Nanking, which was overwhelmed after a two-day siege and was declared the celestial capital of the movement. Fired by the prospect of a golden age, the rebellion now flooded wave upon wave across the whole vast country. More than six thousand citadels were taken by the rebels and occupied for a while; five provinces were razed to the ground in battle after battle; and more than twenty million died in just fifteen years. The bloody horror in China at that time went beyond all imagining. In the summer of 1864, after a seven-year siege by imperial forces, Nanking fell. The defenders had long since exhausted their supplies, and had abandoned all hope of attaining in this life the paradise which had seemed within reach when the movement began. Broken by hunger and drugs, they were on their last legs. On the 30th of June the Celestial King took his own life. Hundreds of thousands followed his example, either out of loyalty to him or for fear of the conquerors' revenge. They committed self-slaughter in every conceivable way, with swords and with knives, by fire, by hanging, or by leaping from the rooftops and towers. Many are even said to have buried themselves alive. The mass suicide of the Taipingis is without historical parallel. When their enemies broke through the gates on the morning of the 19th of July, they found not a soul alive. But the city was filled with the humming of flies. The King of the Celestial Realm of Eternal Peace, according to a despatch sent to Peking, lay face-down in a gutter, his bloated body held together only by the silken robes of imperial yellow, adorned with the image of the dragon, which, with blasphemous presumption, he had always worn.

Suppressing the Taiping rebellion would almost certainly have proved impossible had not the British army contingents in China taken the imperial side after the resolution of their own conflict with the Emperor. The armed presence of the British dated back to 1840, to the beginning of the so-called Opium war. In 1837 the Chinese government had taken measures to prevent opium trading, whereupon the East India Company, which grew opium poppies in the fields of Bengal and shipped the drug mainly to Canton, Amoy and Shanghai, felt that one of its most lucrative ventures was in jeopardy. The subsequent declaration of war began the opening-up, by force of arms, of the Chinese Empire, which for two hundred years had remain closed to foreign barbarians. In the name of Christian evangelism and free trade, which was held to be the precondition of all civilized progress, the superiority of western artillery was demonstrated, a number of cities were stormed, and a peace was extorted, the conditions of which included guarantees for British trading posts on the coast, the cession of Hong Kong, and, not least, reparation payments of truly astronomical proportions. In so far as this arrangement, which from the outset the British regarded as purely interim, made no provision for access to trading centres within China itself, the need for further military campaigns could not be ruled out in the longer term, especially in view of the existence of four hundred million Chinese to whom the cotton fabrics produced in the Lancashire mills might have been sold. It was not, however, until 1856 that an adequate pretext for a new punitive expedition presented itself, when Chinese officials in the port of Canton boarded a freighter to arrest some members of the all-Chinese crew who were suspected of piracy. In the course of this operation, the boarding party hauled down the Union Jack, which was flying from the main mast, probably because at that time the British flag was not infrequently flown as a cover for illegal trafficking. But since the boarded ship was registered in Hong Kong and was flying the Union Jack rightfully, the incident, laughable in itself, provided the representatives of British interests in Canton with the occasion for a confrontation with the Chinese authorities which was presently and deliberately pushed so far that there was felt to be no alternative but to occupy the port and bombard the official residence of the prefect. At very nearly the same time, as luck would have it, the French press was running reports of the execution, on the orders of officials in Kwangsi province, of a missionary named Chapdelaine. The description of this painful procedure culminated in the claim that the executioner had cut the heart from the breast of the dead abbé, and cooked and eaten it. The cries for retaliation and punishment which promptly filled France chimed perfectly with the endeavours of the warmongers in Westminster, so that, once the necessary preparations had been made, there was witnessed the spectacle of a joint Anglo-French campaign, a rare phenomenon in the age of imperial rivalry. This enterprise, which was dogged by the greatest of logistical difficulties, entered its crucial phase in August 1860 with the landing of eighteen thousand British and French troops in the Bay of Pechili, barely a hundred and fifty miles from Peking. Supported by a Chinese auxiliary force recruited in Canton, they captured the forts of Taku that stood surrounded by deep ditches, immense earthworks and bamboo palisades amidst saltwater marshes at the mouth of the Peiho river. After the fortress garrison had unconditionally surrendered and attempts were being made to put an orderly end, by negotiation, to a campaign that had already been concluded from a military point of view, the allied delegates, despite the fact that they had the upper hand, became ever more lost in a nightmarish maze of diplomatic prevarication dictated partly by the complex requirements of protocol in the dragon empire and partly by the fear and bewilderment of the Emperor. In the end, the negotiations foundered on the mutual incomprehension of emissaries from two fundamentally different worlds, a gap which no interpreter could bridge. While the British and French side viewed the peace they would impose as the first stage in the colonization of a moribund realm untouched by the intellectual and material achievements of civilization, the Emperor's delegates, for their part, endeavoured to make clear to these strangers, who appeared to be unfamiliar with Chinese ways, the immemorial obligations toward the Son of Heaven of envoys from satellite powers bound to pay homage and tribute. In the end, there was nothing for it but to sail up the Peiho in gunboats and advance on Peking overland. Emperor Hsien-feng, who was debilitated despite his youthful years and suffered from dropsy, shirked the impending confrontation, departing on the 22nd of September for his retreat at Jehol beyond the Great Wall amidst a disorderly array of court eunuchs, mules, baggage carts, litters and palanquins. Word was conveyed to the commanders of the enemy forces that his majesty the Emperor was obliged by law to go hunting in autumn. In early October the allied troops, themselves now uncertain how to proceed, happened apparently by chance on the magic garden of Yuan Ming Yuan near Peking, with its countless palaces, pavilions, covered walks, fantastic arbours, temples and towers. On the slopes of man-made mountains, between banks and spinneys, deer with fabulous antlers grazed, and the whole incomprehensible glory of Nature and of the wonders placed in it by the hand of man was reflected in dark, unruffled waters. The destruction that was wrought in these legendary landscaped gardens over the next few days, which made a mockery of military discipline or indeed of all reason, can only be understood as resulting from anger at the continued delay in achieving a resolution. Yet the true reason why Yuan Ming Yuan was laid waste may well have been that this earthly paradise – which immediately annihilated any notion of the Chinese as an inferior and uncivilized race – was an irresistible provocation in the eyes of soldiers who, a world away from their homeland, knew nothing but the rule of force, privation, and the abnegation of their own desires. Although the accounts of what happened in those October days are not very reliable, the sheer fact that booty was later auctioned off in the British camp suggests that much of the removable ornaments and the jewellery left behind by the fleeing court, everything made of jade or gold, silver or silk, fell into the hands of the looters. When the summerhouses, hunting lodges and sacred places in the extensive gardens and neighbouring palace precincts, more than two hundred in number, were then burnt to the ground, it was on the orders of the commanding officers, ostensibly in reprisal for the mistreatment of the British emissaries Loch and Parkes, but in reality so that the devastation already wrought should no longer be apparent. The temples, palaces and hermitages, mostly built of cedarwood, went up in flames one after another with unbelievable speed, according to Charles George Gordon, a thirty-year-old captain in the Royal Engineers, the fire spreading through the green shrubs and woods, crackling and leaping. Apart from a few stone bridges and marble pagodas, all was destroyed. For a long time, swathes of smoke drifted over the entire area, and a great cloud of ash that obscured the sun was borne to Peking by the west wind, where after a time it settled on the heads and homes of those who, it was surmised, had been visited by the power of divine retribution. At the end of the month, with the example of Yuan Ming Yuan before them, the Emperor's officers felt obliged to sign without further ado the oft-deferred Treaty of Tientsin. The principal clauses, apart from fresh reparation demands that could scarcely be met, related to the rights of free movement and unhindered missionary activity in the interior of China and to negotiation of a customs tariff with a view to legalizing the opium trade. In return, the Western powers declared themselves willing to uphold the dynasty, which meant putting down the Taiping rebellion and crushing the secessionary movements of the Moslem population of the Shensi, Yunnan and Kansu valley regions, in the course of which between six and ten million people were made homeless or killed. Charles George Gordon, by nature shy and Christian-spirited, though also an irascible and profoundly melancholy man, who was later to die a famous death in the siege of Khartoum, took over the command of the demoralized imperial army and within a short period transformed them into so powerful a fighting force that when he left the country he was invested with the Chinese Empire's highest decoration in recognition of his services, the yellow jacket.

In August 1861, after months of irresolution, Emperor Hsien-feng lay in his Jehol exile approaching the end of his short and dissipated life. The waters had already risen from his abdomen to his heart, and the cells of his gradually dissolving flesh floated like fish in the sea in the salt fluid that leaked from his bloodstream into every available space in the body tissue. Through his flickering consciousness, Hsien-feng followed the invasion by foreign powers of the provinces of his empire by perfect proxy, as his own limbs died off and his organs flooded with toxins. He himself was now the battlefield on which the downfall of China was being accomplished, till on the 22nd of the month the shades of night settled upon him and he sank away wholly into the delirium of death. Because of the precisely ordained procedures to which the Emperor's body had to be subjected before being placed in its coffin, procedures which were linked to complex astrological calculations, transfer of his corpse to Peking could not be arranged before the 5th of October. It then took three weeks for the cortège, more than a mile long, to make the journey, in evenly falling autumn rain, up hill and down dale, through black valleys and gorges and across bleak mountain passes blurred to sight by icy-grey blizzards. The catafalque, which time and again threatened to topple over, was borne on a huge golden bier on the shoulders of a hundred and twenty-four hand-picked pallbearers. On the morning of the 1st of November, when the cortège reached its destination, the road leading to the gates of the Forbidden City had been strewn with yellow sand and screens of blue Nanking silk were positioned on either side to prevent the common people from looking upon the countenance of the five-year-old child Emperor T'ung-chih, whom Hsien-feng had named as his successor to the dragon throne in the last days of his life and who was now being taken homeward on a padded palanquin behind the mortal remains of his father, together with his mother Tz'u-hsi, who had risen from the ranks of concubines and even now had assumed the illustrious title of Dowager Empress. Following the return to court in Peking, the struggle for the powers of regency during the interregnum which inevitably ensued since the heir to the dragon throne was not yet of age, was soon resolved in favour of the widow, whose craving for power was insatiable. The princes who had acted as Hsien-feng's viceroys during his absence were accused of conspiracy against the legitimate ruler, a crime for which there was no defence, and they were condemned to be dismembered and cut into slices. When this sentence was commuted and the traitors were granted permission, offered to them in the form of a silken rope, to hang themselves, it was seen as a token of merciful clemency in the new regime. Once Princes Cheng, Su-shun and Yi had availed themselves of this prerogative, seemingly without any hesitation, the Dowager Empress was the uncontested locum of the Chinese Empire, at least until the time when her son became old enough to rule himself and began taking measures that ran counter to the plans she had nurtured to extend and perfect her power, plans of which many had already been put into practice. Given this turn of events, it was tantamount to providential, from Tz'u-hsi's point of view, that, a scant year after coming to the throne, T'ung-chih was so weakened – by smallpox or by some other disease he had picked up, as rumour had it, from the dancers and transvestites of Peking's streets of sin – that when the planet Venus crossed before the sun in the autumn of 1874, a grim omen, there were fears for his life at the age of barely nineteen. And indeed T'ung-chih did die, a few weeks later, on the 12th of January 1875. His face was turned to the south and for the journey into the beyond he was enrobed in the vestments of eternal life. The funeral obsequies had scarcely been completed in the prescribed form when the wife of the departed Emperor, seventeen years old and several months pregnant according to various sources, poisoned herself with a massive dose of opium. The official version, that her mysterious death was due to the unassuagable grief that had overwhelmed her, could not entirely dispel the suspicion that the young Empress had been got out of the way in order to prolong the regency of the Dowager Empress Tz'u-hsi, who now consolidated her position by having her two-year-old nephew Kuang-hsu proclaimed heir to the throne, a manoeuvre which flew in the face of tradition since Kuang-hsu was of the same generation as T'ung-chih in the lineage of descent, and thus, under an incontrovertible Confucian rule, unentitled to proffer the services of reverence and mourning which were owed the dead man that his spirit might be appeased. The way the Dowager Empress, in other respects extremely conservative in her views, contrived to flout the most venerable precepts when it became necessary, was one sign of her craving for absolute power, which grew more ruthless with every year that passed. And like all absolute rulers, she was concerned to display her exalted position to the world at large and to herself by a lavishness beyond comparison. Her private household alone, managed by senior eunuch Li Lien-ying, standing to her right in this picture,

went through a truly appalling annual sum of six million pounds sterling. The more ostentatious the demonstrations of her authority became, however, the more the fear of losing the infinite power she had so insidiously acquired grew within her. Unable to sleep, she roamed the bizarre shadow landscapes of the palace gardens, amidst the artificial crags, the groves of ferns, and the dark arborvitaes and cypresses. In the early morning she swallowed a pearl ground to powder, as an elixir of invulnerability. She took the greatest of pleasure in lifeless things, and by day would sometimes stand for hours at the windows of her apartments, staring out upon the silent lake to the north, which resembled a painting. The tiny figures of the gardeners in the distant lily fields, or those of the courtiers who skated on the blue ice in winter, did not recall to her the natural occupations and feelings of human kind, but were rather, like flies in a jamjar, already in the wanton power of death. Travellers who were in China between 1876 and 1879 report that, in the drought that had continued for years, whole provinces gave the impression of expiring under prisons of glass. Between seven and twenty million people – no precise estimates have ever been calculated – are said to have died of starvation and exhaustion, principally in Shansi, Shensi and Shantung. A Baptist preacher named Timothy Richard, for example, noted that one effect of the catastrophe, which grew more apparent week by week, was that all movement was slowing down. Singly, in groups and in straggling lines, people tottered across the country, and the merest breath of air might suffice to topple them and leave them lying by the wayside forever. Simply raising a hand, closing an eyelid, or exhaling one's last breath might take, it sometimes seemed, half a century. And as time dissolved, so too did all other relations. Parents exchanged children because they could not bear to watch the dying torment of their own. Towns and villages were surrounded by deserts of dust, over which trembling mirages of river valleys and forested lakes often appeared. Sometimes at first light, when the rustling of leaves dry on the branch penetrated their shallow sleep, people imagined, for a fraction of a second in which wishful thinking was stronger than what they knew to be the case, that it had started to rain. Though the capital and its environs were spared the worst consequences of the drought, when the ill tidings arrived from the south, the Dowager Empress had a daily blood sacrifice offered in her temple to the gods of silk, at the hour when the evening star rose, lest the silkworms want for fresh green leaves. Of all living creatures, these curious insects alone aroused a strong affection in her. The silk houses they were raised in were among the finest buildings of the summer palace. Every day that came, Tz'u-hsi walked the airy halls with the ladies of her retinue, clad in white pinafores, to inspect the progress of the work, and when night fell she particularly liked to sit all alone amidst the frames, listening to the low, even, deeply soothing sound of the countless silkworms consuming the new mulberry foliage. These pale, almost transparent creatures, which would presently give their lives for the fine thread they were spinning, she saw as her true loyal followers. To her they seemed the ideal subjects, diligent in service, ready to die, capable of multiplying vastly within a short span of time, and fixed on their one sole preordained aim, wholly unlike human beings, on whom there was basically no relying, neither on the nameless masses in the empire nor on those who constituted the inmost circle about her and who, she suspected, might go over at any time to the side of the second child Emperor she had installed. Kuang-hsu, who was fascinated by the mysteries of modern machines, spent most of his time taking apart the mechanical toys and clocks sold by a Danish tradesman in his Peking shop, and it was still possible to distract his awakening ambition by promising him a real railway train which he would be able to ride across his own country but the day was not long remote when his would be the power which she, the Dowager Empress, was ever less able to relinquish the longer she possessed it. As I imagine it, the little court train with the image of the Chinese dragon that later served the line from Halesworth to Southwold was originally ordered for Kuang-hsu, and the order was subsequently cancelled in the mid-1890s when the young Emperor began to espouse, in opposition to Tz'u-hsi, the causes of the reform movement under whose influence he had fallen, causes that ran counter to her own purposes. What we do have on authority is that Kuang-hsu's attempts to wrest power to himself ultimately led to his being imprisoned in one of the moated palaces in the Forbidden City, where he was forced to abdicate and make over the power of government, without reservation, to the Dowager Empress. For ten years Kuang-hsu languished in exile on his paradisical island until in the late summer of 1908, the various ailments that increasingly troubled him since the day of his deposition – chronic headaches and backache, renal cramps, hypersensitivity to light and noise, weak lungs, and severe depression – finally overcame him. One Dr Chu, who was familiar with western medicine and was the last to be consulted, diagnosed Bright's disease but also noted a number of inconsistent symptoms – palpitations of the heart, an empurpled complexion, a yellow tongue – that suggest, as has since been speculated, that Kuang-hsu was being gradually poisoned. Visiting the patient in his imperial apartments, Dr Chu noticed moreover that the floors and all the furnishings were thick with dust, as if the house had been long since deserted, an indication that no one had attended to the Emperor's needs for years. On the 14th of November 1908 at dusk, or, as they say, at the hour of the cockerel, Kuang-hsu, racked with pain, departed this life. At the time of his death he was thirty-seven years old. Strangely enough, the seventy-three-year-old Dowager Empress, who had destroyed his body and his spirit with such persistent intent, outlived him by less than a day. On the morning of the 15th of November, still in reasonably good health, she presided over the grand council's deliberations upon the new situation, but after her midday meal, which in defiance of her personal doctors' warnings she had concluded with a double helping of her favourite pudding – crab apples with clotted cream – she was stricken with an attack resembling dysentery, from which she did not recover. She died at about three o'clock. Already draped in her shroud, she dictated her farewell to the Empire which now after the near half century of her regency was in the throes of dissolution. Looking back, she said, she realized that history consists of nothing but misfortune and the troubles that afflict us, so that in all our days on earth we never know one single moment that is genuinely free of fear.

The denial of time, so the tract on Orbius Tertius tells us, is one of the key tenets of the philosophical schools of Tlön. According to this principle, the future exists only in the shape of our present apprehensions and hopes, and the past merely as memory. In a different view, the world and everything now living in it was created only moments ago, together with its complete but illusory pre-history. A third school of thought variously describes our earth as a cul-de-sac in the great city of God, a dark cave crowded with incomprehensible images, or a hazy aura surrounding a better sun. The advocates of a fourth philosophy maintain that time has run its course and that this life is no more than the fading reflection of an event beyond recall. We simply do not know how many of its possible mutations the world may already have gone through, or how much time, always assuming that it exists, remains. All that is certain is that night lasts far longer than day, if one compares an individual life, life as a whole, or time itself with the system which, in each case, is above it. The night of time, wrote Thomas Browne in his treatise of 1658, *The Garden of Cyrus,* far surpasseth the day and who knows when was the Aequinox? – Thoughts of this kind were in my head too as I walked on along the disused railway line a little way beyond the bridge across the Blyth, and then dropped from the higher ground to the level of the marsh that extends southward from Walberswick as far as Dunwich, which now consists of a few houses only. The region is so empty and deserted that, if one were abandoned there, one could scarcely say whether one was on the North Sea coast or perhaps by the Caspian Sea or the Gulf of Lian-tung. With the rippling reeds to my right and the grey beach to my left, I pressed on toward Dunwich, which seemed so far in the distance as to be quite beyond my reach.

It was as if I had been walking for hours before the tiled roofs of houses and the crest of a wooded hill gradually became defined. The Dunwich of the present day is what remains of a town that was one of the most important ports in Europe in the Middle Ages. There were more than fifty churches, monasteries and convents, and hospitals here; there were shipyards and fortifications and a fisheries and merchant fleet of eighty vessels; and there were dozens of windmills. All of it has gone under, quite literally, and is now below the sea, beneath alluvial sand and gravel, over an area of two or three square miles. The parish churches of St James, St Leonard, St Martin, St Bartholomew, St Michael, St Patrick, St Mary, St John, St Peter, St Nicholas and St Felix, one after the other, toppled down the steadily receding cliff-face and sank in the depths, along with the earth and stone of which the town had been built. All that survived, strange to say, were the walled well shafts, which for centuries, freed of that which had once enclosed them, rose aloft like the chimney stacks of some subterranean smithy, as various chroniclers report, until in due course these symbols of the vanished town also fell down. Until about 1890 what was known as Eccles Church Tower still stood on Dunwich beach,

and no one had any idea how it had arrived at sea level, from the considerable height at which it must once have stood, without tipping out of the perpendicular. The riddle has not been solved to this day, though a recent experiment using a model suggests that the enigmatic Eccles Tower was probably built on sand and sank down under its own weight, so gradually that the masonry remained virtually intact. Around 1900, after Eccles Tower had also collapsed, the only Dunwich church that remained was the ruin of All Saints.

In 1919 it, too, slipped over the cliff edge, together with the bones of those buried in the churchyard, and only the square west tower still rose for a time above those eerie parts. Dunwich reached the high point of its evolution in the thirteenth century. Every day, in those times, the ships came and went, to London, Stavoren, Stralsund, Danzig, Bruges, Bayonne and Bordeaux. A quarter of the great fleet that sailed from Portsmouth in May 1230, bearing hundreds of knights and their horses, several thousand foot soldiers, and the entire royal entourage, came from Dunwich. Shipbuilding, and the trade in timber, grain, salt, herring, wool and hides, were so profitable that the town was soon in a position to build every conceivable kind of defence against attack from the landward side and against the force of the sea, which was ceaselessly eroding the coast. One cannot say how great was the sense of security which the people of Dunwich derived from the building of these fortifications. All we know for certain is that they ultimately proved inadequate. On New Year's Eve 1285, a storm tide devastated the lower town and the portside so terribly that for months afterwards no one could tell where the land ended and the sea began. There were fallen walls, debris, ruins, broken timbers, shattered ships' hulls, and sodden masses of loam, pebbles, sand and water everywhere. And then on the 14th of January 1328, after only a few decades of rebuilding, and following an autumn and Christmas period that had been unusually tranquil, an even more fearful disaster occurred, if such were possible. Once again, a hurricane-force north-easterly storm coincided with the highest tide of the month. As darkness fell, those living around the harbour fled with whatever belongings they could carry to the upper town. All night the waves clawed away one row of houses after another. Like mighty battering rams the roofing and supporting beams adrift in the water smashed against the walls that had not yet been levelled. When dawn came, the throng of survivors – numbering some two or three thousand, among them gentry such as the FitzRicharts, the FitzMaurices, the Valeins and the de la Falaises as well as the common people – stood on the edge of the abyss, leaning into the wind, gazing in horror through the clouds of salt spray into the depths where bales and barrels, shattered cranes, torn sails of windmills, chests and tables, crates, feather beds, firewood, straw and drowned livestock were revolving in a whirlpool of whitish-brown waters. Over the centuries that followed, catastrophic incursions of the sea into the land of this kind happened time and again, and, even during long years of apparent calm, coastal erosion continued to take its natural course. Little by little the people of Dunwich accepted the inevitability of the process. They abandoned their hopeless struggle, turned their backs on the sea, and, whenever their declining means allowed it, built to the westward in a protracted flight that went on for generations; the slowly dying town thus followed – by reflex, one might say – one of the fundamental patterns of human behaviour. A strikingly large number of our settlements are oriented to the west and, where circumstances permit, relocate in a westward direction. The east stands for lost causes. Especially at the time when the continent of America was being colonized, it was noticeable that the townships spread to the west even as their eastern districts were falling apart. In Brazil, to this day, whole provinces die down like fires when the land is exhausted by overcropping and new areas to the west are opened up. In North America, too, countless settlements of various kinds, complete with gas stations, motels and shopping malls, move west along the turnpikes, and along that axis affluence and squalor are unfailingly polarized. I was put in mind of this phenomenon by the flight of Dunwich. After the first serious disaster, building began on the westernmost fringe of the town, but even of the Grey Friars monastery that dates from that time only a few fragments now remain. Dunwich, with its towers and many thousand souls, has dissolved into water, sand and thin air. If you look out from the cliff-top across the sea towards where the town must once have been, you can sense the immense power of emptiness. Perhaps it was for this reason that Dunwich became a place of pilgrimage for melancholy poets in the Victorian age. Algernon Charles Swinburne, for instance, went there on several occasions in the 1870s with his companion Theodore Watts-Dunton, whenever the excitement of London literary life threatened to overtax his nerves, which had been hypersensitive since his early childhood. He had achieved legendary fame as a young man, and many a time he had been sent into such impassioned paroxysms by the dazzling conversations on art in the Pre-Raphaelite salons, or by the mental strain of composing his own verse and tragedies, overflowing with wonderful poetic bombast, that he could no longer control his own voice and limbs. After these quasi-epileptic fits he often lay prostrate for weeks, and soon, unfitted for general society, he could bear only the company of those who were close to him. Initially he spent the periods of convalescence at the family country estate, but later, ever more frequently, he went to the coast with the trusty Watts-Dunton. Rambles from Southwold to Dunwich, through the windblown fields of sedge, worked like a sedative upon him. A long poem entitled *By the North Sea* was his tribute to the gradual dissolution of life. Like ashes the low cliffs crumble and the banks drop down into dust. I remember reading in a study of Swinburne that, one summer evening, when he was visiting the churchyard of All Saints with Watts-Dunton, he thought he saw a greenish glow far out on the surface of the sea. The glow, he is reported as saying, reminded him of the palace of Kublai Khan, which was built on the site later occupied by Peking at the very time when Dunwich was one of the most important communities in the kingdom of England. If I remember rightly, that same study told how Swinburne described every last detail of the fabled palace to Watts-Dunton that evening: the snow-white wall more than four miles in length, the arsenals crammed with bridles, saddles and armour of every sort, the storehouses and treasuries, the stables where row upon row of the finest horses stood, the banqueting halls that could accommodate more than six thousand, the private apartments, the zoo with its unicorn enclosure, and the hill, three hundred feet high, that the Khan had caused to be raised on the north side, in order to command an unrestricted view. Within the space of a year, Swinburne reputedly said, this new landmark, the slopes of which were strewn with green malachite, was planted with the rarest and most majestic of mature evergreen trees, which had been dug up complete with roots and earth from where they originally grew and transported, often over considerable distances, by specially trained teams of elephants. Never before, Swinburne is said to have claimed that evening in Dunwich, nor ever since, had anything more beautiful been created on earth than that artificial hill, which was green even in midwinter and crowned by a palace of peace, in a similar hue of green. Algernon Charles Swinburne, whose life was coterminous to the year with that of the Dowager Empress Tz'u-hsi, was born on the 5th of April 1837, the eldest of the six children of Admiral Charles Henry Swinburne and his wife, Lady Jane Henrietta, daughter of the third Earl of Ashburnham. Both families traced their ancestry to that remote time when Kublai Khan was building his palace and Dunwich was trading with every nation that could then be reached by sea. As long as anyone could remember, the Swinburnes and the Ashburnhams had been members of the royal entourage, prominent commanders and warriors, lords of vast estates, and explorers. Curious to relate, one General Robert Swinburne, great uncle to Algernon Swinburne, became a subject of His Apostolic Majesty and was invested a Baron of the Holy Roman Empire, presumably on the strength of his pronounced ultramontane leanings. When he died he was governor of Milan, and his son, until his death in 1907 at the age of eighty-seven, held the office of chamberlain to Kaiser Franz Josef. This extreme manifestation of political Catholicism in one branch of the family may conceivably have been a first sign of decadence. That aside, however, the question remains of how a family so adept at life should have produced a scion forever on the verge of a nervous breakdown, a paradox which long puzzled Swinburne's biographers as they eagerly teased at his family descent and hereditary make-up, till at length they agreed to describe the poet of *Atalanta in Calydon* as an epigenetic phenomenon sprung from the void, as it were, from beyond all natural possibility. It is certain that Swinburne, by reason of his physical appearance alone, must have seemed a complete aberration.

He was small of stature, and at every point in his development he had remained far behind a normal size; he was quite startlingly fine-limbed; yet even as a boy he had an extraordinarily large, indeed outsize, head on his shoulders, which sloped weakly away from his neck. That truly unusual head, which was made the more striking by his bushy, fiery-red shock of hair and his piercing, watery-green eyes, made Swinburne, as one of his contemporaries noted, an object of amazement at Eton. On the day that he started school – it was the summer of 1849, and Swinburne had just turned twelve – his was the largest hat in all Eton. A certain Lindo Myers, together with whom Swinburne later crossed the Channel from Le Havre in the autumn of 1868, on which occasion a gust of wind blew the hat off Swinburne's head and swept it overboard, writes that after they docked in Southampton it was not until the third purveyor of hats that they found headgear to fit Swinburne, and even then, Myers adds, the leather band and the lining had to be removed. Despite his extremely ill-proportioned physique, Swinburne dreamt from early youth, and particularly after reading newspaper accounts of the charge at Balaclava, of joining a cavalry regiment and losing his life as a *beau sabreur* in some equally senseless battle. Even when he was a student at Oxford, this vision outshone any other conception he might have of his own future; and only when all hope of dying a hero's death was gone, thanks to his underdeveloped body, did he devote himself unreservedly to literature and thus, perhaps, to a no less radical form of self-destruction. Possibly Swinburne would not have survived the nervous crises which became more serious as time went on, had he not increasingly submitted to the regime of his lifetime companion, Watts-Dunton. Watts-Dunton was soon attending to the entire correspondence, dealing with all the little matters that were continuously putting Swinburne into the utmost panic, and thus made it possible for the poet to eke out almost three more decades of pallid afterlife. In 1879, more dead than alive following a nervous attack, Swinburne was taken in a four-wheeler to Putney Hill in south-west London, and there, at number 2, The Pines, a modest suburban town house, the two

bachelors lived henceforth, carefully avoiding the least excitement. Their days invariably followed a routine devised by Watts-Dunton. Swinburne, Watts-Dunton reportedly said with a certain pride in the tried and tested correctness of his system, always walks in the morning, writes in the afternoon and reads in the evening. And, what is more, at meal times he eats like a caterpillar and at night he sleeps like a dormouse. Now and then a guest who wished to see the prodigious poet in his suburban exile was invited to lunch. The three would then sit at the table in the gloomy dining room, Watts-Dunton, who was hard of hearing, making conversation in booming tones while Swinburne, like a well-brought-up child, kept his head bowed over his plate, devouring an enormous helping of beef in silence. One of the visitors to Putney at the turn of the century wrote that the two old gentlemen put him in mind of strange insects in a Leiden jar. Time and again, looking at Swinburne, this visitor continued, he was reminded of the ashy grey silkworm, *Bombyx mori*, be it because of how he munched his way through his food bit by bit or be it because, out of the snooze he had slipped into after lunch, he abruptly awoke to new life, convulsed with electric energy, and, flapping his hands flitted about his library, like a startled moth, clambering up and down the stands and ladders to fetch the one or other treasure from the shelves. The enthusiasm which seized him as he was thus engaged found expression in rhapsodic declamations about his favourite poets Marlowe, Landor and Hugo, but also in not infrequent reminiscences of his childhood on the Isle of Wight and in Northumberland. In one such moment, in utter rapture, he apparently recalled sitting at his old Aunt Ashburnham's feet as a boy, listening to her account of the first grand ball she went to as a girl, accompanied by her mother. After the ball they drove many miles homeward on a crisp, cold, snow-bright winter night, when suddenly the carriage stopped by a group of dark figures who, it transpired, were burying a suicide at a crossroads. In writing down this memory that goes back a century and a half into the past, noted the visitor, himself long since deceased, he beheld perfectly clearly the dreadful Hogarthian nocturne as Swinburne painted it, and the little boy too, with his big head and fiery hair standing on end, wringing his hands and beseeching: Tell me more, Aunt Ashburnham, please tell me more.

VII

It had grown uncommonly sultry and dark when at midday, after resting on the beach, I climbed to Dunwich Heath, which lies forlorn above the sea. The history of how that melancholy region came to be is closely connected not only with the nature of the soil and the influence of a maritime climate but also, far more decisively, with the steady and advancing destruction, over a period of many centuries and indeed millennia, of the dense forests that extended over the entire British Isles after the last Ice Age. In Norfolk and Suffolk, it was chiefly oaks and elms that grew on the flatlands, spreading in unbroken waves across the gently undulating country right down to the coast. This phase of evolution was halted when the first settlers burnt off the forests along those drier stretches of the eastern coast where the light soil could be tilled. Just as the woods had once colonized the earth in irregular patterns, gradually growing together, so ever more extensive fields of ash and cinders now ate their way into that green-leafed world in a similarly haphazard fashion. If today one flies over the Amazon basin or over Borneo and sees the mountainous palls of smok hanging, seemingly motionless, over the forest canopy, which from above resembles a mere patch of moss, then perhaps one can imagine what those fires, which sometimes burned on for months, would leave in their wake. Whatever was spared by the flames in prehistoric Europe was later felled for construction and shipbuilding, and to make the charcoal which the smelting of iron required in vast quantities. By the seventeenth century, only a few insignificant remnants of the erstwhile forests survived in the islands, most of them untended and decaying. The great fires were now lit on the other side of the ocean. It is not for nothing that Brazil owes its name to the French word for charcoal. Our spread over the earth was fuelled by reducing the higher species of vegetation to charcoal, by incessantly burning whatever would burn. From the first smouldering taper to the elegant lanterns whose light reverberated around eighteenth-century courtyards and from the mild radiance of these lanterns to the unearthly glow of the sodium lamps that line the Belgian motorways, it has all been combustion. Combustion is the hidden principle behind every artefact we create. The making of a fish-hook, manufacture of a china cup, or production of a television programme, all depend on the same process of combustion. Like our bodies and like our desires, the machines we have devised are possessed of a heart which is slowly reduced to embers. From the earliest times, human civilization has been no more than a strange luminescence growing more intense by the hour, of which no one can say when it will begin to wane and when it will fade away. For the time being, our cities still shine through the night, and the fires still spread. In Italy, France and Spain, in Hungary, Poland and Lithuania, in Canada and

California, summer fires consume whole forests, not to mention the great conflagration in the tropics that is never extinguished. A few years ago, on a Greek island that was wooded as recently as 1900, I observed the speed with which a blaze runs through dry vegetation. A short distance from the harbour town where I was staying, I stood by the roadside with a group of agitated men, the blackness behind us and before us, far below at the bottom of a gorge, the fire, whipped up by the wind, racing, leaping, and already climbing the steep slopes. And I shall never forget the junipers, dark against the glow, going up in flames one after the other as if they were tinder the moment the first tongues of fire licked at them, with a dull thudding sound like an explosion, and then promptly collapsing in a silent shower of sparks.

My way from Dunwich took me at first by the ruins of the Grey Friars' monastery, through a number of fields, and then to an overgrown scrubland where stunted pines, birches and rampant gorse grew so densely that the going was very hard. I was beginning to think of turning back when all of a sudden the heath opened out in front of me. Shading from pale lilac to deepest purple, it stretched away westward, with a white track curving gently through its midst. Lost in the thoughts that went round in my head incessantly, and numbed by this crazed flowering, I stuck to the sandy path until to my astonishment, not to say horror, I found myself back again at the same tangled thicket from which I had emerged about an hour before, or, as it now seemed to me, in some distant past. Only in retrospect did I realize that the only discernible landmark on this treeless heath, a most peculiar villa with a glass-domed observation tower which reminded me somehow of Ostend, had presented itself time and again from a quite different angle, now close to, now further off, now to my left and now to my right, and indeed at one point the lookout tower, in a sort of castling move, had got itself, in no time at all, from one side of the building to the other, so that it seemed that instead of seeing the actual villa I was seeing its mirror image. Moreover, my sense of confusion was deepened by the fact that the signposts at the forks and crossings of the tracks gave no directions to any place or its distance; there was invariably, to my mounting irritation, no more than a mute arrow facing pointlessly this way or that. If one obeyed one's instincts, the path would sooner or later diverge further and further from the goal one was aiming to reach. Simply walking straight ahead cross-country was out of the question on account of the heather, which was woody and knee-deep, so that I had no choice but to keep to the crooked sandy tracks and to make mental notes of even the least significant features, even the slightest shift in perspective. Several times I was forced to retrace long stretches in that bewildering terrain, which could perhaps be surveyed in its entirety only from the glass tower of that spectral Belgian villa. In the end I was overcome by a feeling of panic. The low, leaden sky; the sickly violet hue of the heath clouding the eye; the silence, which rushed in the ears like the sound of the sea in a shell; the flies buzzing about me – all this became oppressive and unnerving. I cannot say how long I walked about in that state of mind, or how I found a way out. But I do remember that suddenly I stood on a country lane, beneath a mighty oak, and the horizon was spinning all around as if I had jumped off a merry-go-round. Months after this experience, which I still cannot explain, I was on Dunwich Heath once more in a dream, walking the endlessly winding paths again, and again I could not find my way out of the maze which I was convinced had been created solely for me. Dead tired and ready to lie down anywhere, as dusk fell I gained a raised area where a little Chinese pavilion had been built, as in the middle of the yew maze at Somerleyton. And when I looked down from this vantage point I saw the labyrinth, the light sandy ground, the sharply delineated contours of hedges taller than a man and almost pitch-black now – a pattern simple in comparison with the tortuous trail I had behind me, but one which I knew in my dream, with absolute certainty, represented a cross-section of my brain.

Beyond the maze, shadows were drifting across the brume of the heath, and then, one by one, the stars came out from the depths of space. Night, the astonishing, the stranger to all that is human, over the mountain-tops mournful and gleaming draws on. It was as though I stood at the topmost point of the earth, where the glittering winter sky is forever unchanging; as though the heath were rigid with frost, and adders, vipers and lizards of transparent ice lay slumbering in their hollows in the sand. From my resting place in the pavilion I gazed out across the heath into the night. And I saw that, to the south, entire headlands had broken off the coast and sunk beneath the waves. The Belgian villa was already teetering over the precipice, while in the cockpit of the lookout tower a corpulent figure in captain's uniform was busying himself at a battery of searchlights, the beams of which, probing the darkness, reminded me of the War. Although in my dream I was sitting transfixed with amazement in the Chinese pavilion, I was at the same time out in the open, within a foot of the very edge, and knew how fearful it is to cast one's eye so low. The crows and choughs that winged the midway air were scarce the size of beetles; the fishermen that walked upon the beach appeared like mice; and the murmuring surge that chafed the countless pebbles could not be heard so high. Immediately below the cliff, on a black heap of earth, were the shattered ruins of a house. Wedged in among the remains of walls, broken chests of drawers, banisters, upended bathtubs and buckled heating pipes were the strangely contorted bodies of those people who had lived there and who, only moments before, had gone to sleep in their beds. A little way off from this scene of devastation, a solitary old man with a wild mane of hair was kneeling beside his dead daughter, both of them so tiny, as if on a stage a mile off. No last sigh, no last words were to be heard, nor the last despairing plea: Lend me a looking-glass;

if that her breath will mist or stain the stone, why, then she lives. No, nothing. Nothing but dead silence. Then softly, barely audibly, the sound of a funeral march. Now night is almost over and the dawn about to break. The contours of the Sizewell power plant, its Magnox block a glowering mausoleum, begin to loom upon an island far out in the pallid waters where one believes the Dogger Bank to be, where once the shoals of herring spawned and earlier still, a long, long time ago, the delta of the Rhine flowed out into the sea and where green forests grew from silting sands.

Some two hours after my fortuitous release from the labyrinth of the heath, I reached the village of Middleton, where I planned to visit the writer Michael Hamburger, who has lived there for almost twenty years. It was nearly four o'clock. Neither in the village street nor in the gardens was there a soul in sight, the houses gave an unwelcoming impression, and, with my hat in my hand and my rucksack over my shoulder, I felt like a journeyman in a century gone by, so out of place that I should not have been surprised if a band of street urchins had come skipping after me or one of Middleton's householders had stepped out upon his threshold to tell me to be on my way. After all, every foot traveller incurs the suspicion of the locals, especially nowadays, and particularly if he does not fit the image of a local rambler. Perhaps that was why the blue-eyed girl in the village shop gave me such a flabbergasted stare. The jingle of the door bell had long since faded, and I had been standing for a while in the little grocer's shop, which was piled to the ceiling with tinned foods and other imperishables, when she emerged from a back room, where the light of a television flickered, to gape at me with her mouth half open, as if I had landed from another planet. Once she had recovered somewhat, she scrutinized me with a disapproving air, her eye fixing at length on my dusty footwear, and when I wished her a good afternoon she again stared at me, utterly stunned. It has often struck me that when country people set eyes on a foreigner they are quite overawed, and, even if he has a good command of their language, they find it hard to understand him. The girl in Middleton village shop was no exception, and merely shook her head nervously when I asked for mineral water. What she at length sold me was an ice-cold can of Cherry Coke, which I drained at a draught like a cup of hemlock, leaning against the churchyard wall, before walking the last few hundred yards to Michael's house.

Michael was nine and a half when, in November 1933, with his siblings, his mother, and her parents, he came to England. His father had already left Berlin several months before, and was installed in one of those unheatable stone houses in Edinburgh, where, wrapped in woollen blankets, he pored over dictionaries and textbooks until late at night; for, despite having been professor of paediatrics at the Charité, he now, in his fifties, had to sit his medical examinations all over again in a language unfamiliar to him if he was to continue in practice as a doctor. Michael later wrote in his memoirs about the fears and anxieties of the family as they travelled toward the unknown, fears which came to a head in the customs hall in Dover as they looked on with horror as Grandfather's pair of budgerigars, which had so far survived the journey unharmed, were impounded. It was the loss of the two pet birds, Michael writes, and having to stand by powerless and see them vanish for ever behind some sort of screen, that brought us up against the whole monstrosity of changing countries under such inauspicious circumstances. The disappearance of those budgerigars at Dover customs marked the beginning of the disappearance of his Berlin childhood behind the new identity that he assumed little by little over the next decade. How little there has remained in me of my native country, the chronicler observes as he scans the few memories he still possesses, barely enough for an obituary of a lost boyhood. The mane of a Prussian lion, a Prussian nanny, caryatids bearing the globe on their shoulders, the mysterious sounds of traffic and motor horns rising from Lietzenburgerstraße to the apartment, the noise made by the central-heating pipe behind the wallpaper in the dark corner where one had to stand facing the wall by way of punishment, the nauseating smell of soapsuds in the laundry, a game of marbles in a Charlottenburg park, barley malt coffee, sugar-beet syrup, cod-liver oil, and the forbidden raspberry sweets from Grandmother Antonina's silver bonbonniere – were these not all merely phantasms, delusions, that had dissolved into thin air? The leather seats in Grandfather's Buick, Hasensprung tramstop in the Grunewald, the Baltic coast, Heringsdorf, a sand dune surrounded by pure nothingness, the sunlight and how it fell . . . Whenever a shift in our spiritual life occurs and fragments such as these surface, we believe we can remember. But in reality, of course, memory fails us. Too many buildings have fallen down, too much rubble has been heaped up, the moraines and deposits are insuperable. If I now look back to Berlin, writes Michael, all I see is a darkened background with a grey smudge in it, a slate pencil drawing, some unclear numbers and letters in a gothic script, blurred and half wiped away with a damp rag. Perhaps this blind spot is also a vestigial image of the ruins through which I wandered in 1947 when I returned to my native city for the first time to search for traces of the life I had lost. For a few days I went about like a sleepwalker, past houses of which only the façades were left standing, smoke-blackened brick walls and fields of rubble along the never-ending streets of Charlottenburg, until one afternoon I unexpectedly found myself in front of the Lietzenburgerstraße building where we had lived and which had escaped destruction – absurdly, as it seemed to me. I can still feel the cold breath of air that brushed my brow as I entered the hallway, and I recall that the cast-iron balustrade on the stairs, the stucco garlands on the walls, the spot where the perambulator had been parked, and the largely unchanged names on the metal letter boxes, appeared to me like pictures in a rebus that I simply had to puzzle out correctly in order to cancel the monstrous events that had happened since we emigrated. It was as if it were now up to me alone, as if by some trifling mental exertion I could reverse the entire course of history, as if – if I desired it only – Grandmother Antonina, who had refused to go with us to England, would still be living in Kantstraße as before; she would not have gone on that journey, of which we had been informed by a Red Cross postcard shortly after the so-called outbreak of War, but would still be concerned about the wellbeing of her goldfish, which she washed under the kitchen tap every day and placed on the window ledge when the weather was fine, for a little fresh air. All that was required was a moment of concentration, piecing together the syllables of the word concealed in the riddle, and everything would again be as it once was. But I could neither make out the word nor bring myself to mount the stairs and ring the bell of our old flat. Instead I left the building with a sick feeling in the pit of my stomach and walked and walked, aimlessly and without being able to grasp even the simplest thought, well past the Westkreuz or the Hallesches Tor or the Tiergarten, I can no longer say where; all I know is that at length I came upon a cleared site where the bricks retrieved from the ruins had been stacked in long, precise rows, ten by ten by ten, a thousand to every stacked cube, or rather nine hundred and ninety-nine, since the thousandth brick in every pile was stood upright on top, be it as a token of expiation or to facilitate the counting. If I now think back to that desolate place, I do not see a single human being, only bricks, millions of bricks, a rigorously perfected system of bricks reaching in serried ranks as far as the horizon, and above them the Berlin November sky from which presently the snow would come swirling down – a deathly silent image of the onset of winter, which I sometimes suspect may have originated in a hallucination, especially when I imagine that out of that endless emptiness I can hear the closing bars of the *Freischütz* overture, and then, without cease, for days and weeks, the scratching of a gramophone needle. My hallucinations and dreams, Michael writes elsewhere, often take place in a setting reminiscent partly of the metropolis of Berlin and partly of rural Suffolk. For instance, I may be standing at a window on the upper floor of our house, but what I see is not the familiar marshes and the willows thrashing as they always do, but rather, from several hundred yards up, acres and acres of allotment gardens bisected by a road, straight as an arrow, down which black taxi cabs speed out of the city in the direction of the Wannsee. Or I am returning at dusk from a long journey. With my rucksack over my shoulder, I walk the last stretch towards our house, in front of which, for some unknown reason, a motley assortment of vehicles is parked, immense limousines, motorized wheelchairs with enormous hand brakes and bulbous horns at the side, and an ominous ivory-coloured ambulance with two deaconesses sitting in it. Under their watchful eyes I hesitantly cross the threshold, and as I do so I no longer know where I am. The rooms are dimly lit, the walls are bare, the furniture is gone. All manner of silver utensils lie on the parquet floor, heavy, ornate knives, spoons and forks as well as fish cutlery for countless people, to dine on a leviathan. Two men in grey linen coats are taking down a tapestry. Crates of china are brimming with wood shavings. In my dream more than an hour goes by before I am able to grasp that I am not in the Middleton house but in the rambling Bleibtreustraße flat where my mother's parents lived, the museum-like rooms of which impressed me very nearly as much, on my childhood visits, as the splendid suites in the palace of Sanssouci. And now they are all gathered here, my Berlin relatives, my German and my English friends, my in-laws, my children, the living and the dead. Unseen by them, I walk through their midst, from one room to another, through galleries, halls and passages thronged with guests until, at the far end of an imperceptibly sloping corridor, I come to the unheated drawing room that used to be known, in our house in Edinburgh, as the Cold Glory. There my father sits, on a stool that is far too low, practising the cello, while Grandmother is lying on a high table, dressed in her best. The gleaming tips of her patent-leather shoes point towards the ceiling, she has spread a grey silk handkerchief over her face, and for days, as always during her regularly recurring bouts of melancholy, she has not uttered a single word. From the window, far off, I see a Silesian landscape. A golden cupola glints from the depth of a valley enclosed by blue forested hills. This is Myslowitz, a place somewhere in Poland, I hear my father say, and as I turn I see the white vapour that had carried his words lingering in the ice-cold air.

The afternoon was well advanced when I reached Michael's house in the meadows on the outskirts of Middleton. I was grateful of the opportunity to rest in the peaceful garden after my wanderings on the heath, which now, in the telling, assumed an air of unreality. Michael had brought out a pot of tea from which there came the occasional puff of steam as from a toy engine. Otherwise, there was not the slightest movement, not even among the grey leaves of the willows in the field beyond the garden. We talked about the deserted, soundless month of August. For weeks, said Michael, there is not a bird to be seen. It is as if everything was somehow hollowed out. Everything is on the point of decline, and only the weeds flourish: bindweed strangles the shrubs, the yellow roots of nettles creep onward in the soil, burdock stands a whole head taller than oneself, brown rot and greenfly are everywhere, and even the sheets of paper on which one endeavours to put together a few words and sentences seem covered in mildew. For days and weeks on end one racks one's brains to no avail, and, if asked, one could not say whether one goes on writing purely out of habit, or a craving for admiration, or because one knows not how to do anything other, or out of sheer wonderment, despair or outrage, any more than one could say whether writing renders one more perceptive or more insane. Perhaps we all lose our sense of reality to the precise degree to which we are engrossed in our own work, and perhaps that is why we see in the increasing complexity of our mental constructs a means for greater understanding, even while intuitively we know that we shall never be able to fathom the imponderables that govern our course through life. Does one follow in Hölderlin's footsteps, simply because one's birthday happened to fall two days after his? Is that why one is tempted time and again to cast reason aside like an old coat, to sign one's poems and letters "your humble servant Scardanelli", and to keep unwelcome guests who come to stare at one at arm's length by addressing them as Your Excellency or Majesty? Does one begin to translate elegies at the age of fifteen or sixteen because one has been exiled from one's homeland? Is it possible that later one would settle in this house in Suffolk because a water pump in the garden bears the date 1770, the year of Hölderlin's birth? For when I heard that one of the near islands was Patmos, I greatly desired there to be lodged, and there to approach the dark grotto. And did Hölderlin not dedicate his Patmos hymn to the Landgrave of Homburg, and was not Homburg also the maiden name of Mother? Across what distances in time do the elective affinities and correspondences connect? How is it that one perceives oneself in another human being, or, if not oneself, then one's own precursor? The fact that I first passed through British customs thirty-three years after Michael, that I am now thinking of giving up teaching as he did, that I am bent over my writing in Norfolk and he in Suffolk, that we both are distrustful of our work and both suffer from an allergy to alcohol – none of these things are particularly strange. But why it was that on my first visit to Michael's house I instantly felt as if I lived or had once lived there, in every respect precisely as he does, I cannot explain. All I know is that I stood spellbound in his high-ceilinged studio room with its north-facing windows in front of the heavy mahogany bureau at which Michael said he no longer worked because the room was so cold, even in midsummer; and that, while we talked of the difficulty of

heating old houses, a strange feeling came upon me, as if it were not he who had abandoned that place of work but I, as if the spectacles cases, letters and writing materials that had evidently lain untouched for months in the soft north light had once been my spectacles cases, my letters and my writing materials. In the porch that led to the garden, I felt again as if I or someone akin to me had long gone about his business there. The wicker baskets full of small twigs for kindling the fire, the polished white and pale grey stones, shells and other seashore finds mutely foregathered on the chest of drawers against the pale blue wall, the jiffy bags and packages stacked in a corner by the pantry door awaiting reuse, all seemed as if they were still lifes created by my own hand. Peering into the pantry, which held a particular fascination for me, my eye

was caught by several jars of preserved fruit that stood on the otherwise empty shelves and by a few dozen diminutive crimson apples on the sill of the window darkened by the yew tree outside. And as I looked on these apples which shone through the half-light much as the golden apples likened in Proverbs to a word fitly spoken, the quite outlandish thought crossed my mind that these things, the kindling, the jiffy bags, the fruit preserves, the seashells and the sound of the sea within them had all outlasted me, and that Michael was taking me round a house in which I myself had lived a long time ago. But thoughts of this kind are dispelled as speedily as they appear. At all events, I did not pursue them in the years that have passed since then, perhaps because it is not possible to pursue them without losing one's sanity. In view of this, I was all the more astonished, when recently I read Michael's memoirs again, to come across a name familiar to me from my time in Manchester, that of Stanley Kerry, which on first reading had eluded me for some reason. Michael relates at this point in his account how, in April 1944, nine months after he joined the Queen's Own Royal West Kent Regiment, he was transferred from Maidstone to Blackburn, Lancashire, where his batallion was quartered in a disused cotton mill. Not long after he arrived in Blackburn he was invited by a fellow soldier to spend Easter Monday at his home in Burnley, a town whose black cobbled streets, derelict factories, and zigzag rooftops of back-to-back houses outlined against the sky like dragons' teeth, made a more forlorn impression on him than anything he had so far seen in England. Curiously enough, twenty-two years later, when in the autumn of 1966 I came from Switzerland to England, my first outing, on All Souls' Day, together with a prospective secondary school teacher, was also to Burnley, or rather to the moors above Burnley. I can see us still, driving back down from the moor in the teacher's little red van, via Burnley and Blackburn to Manchester, as dusk was falling at about four in the afternoon. And not only did my first excursion from Manchester take me to Burnley, where

Michael had been in 1944, but, moreover, the very Stanley Kerry with whom Michael made his trip was one of my first acquaintances in Manchester also. At the time when I took up my teaching post at Manchester university, Stanley Kerry must have been one of the longest-serving lecturers in the German department. He had something of a reputation for eccentricity, owing to his habit of keeping a distance from his colleagues and devoting most of his spare time to the study of the Japanese language. In this he was making astounding progress. When I arrived in Manchester, he had already begun practising his writing skills with brush and pen and would spend many hours in deep concentration drawing one character after another on immense sheets of paper. I recall now how he once said to me that one of the chief difficulties of writing consisted in thinking, with the tip of the pen, solely of the word to be written, whilst banishing from one's mind the reality of what one intends to describe. I remember also that when he made this observation, which applies to poets as well as to pupils in primary school, we were standing in the Japanese garden he had created at the back of his bungalow in Wythenshaw. Evening was drawing in. The banks of moss and the stones were beginning to grow darker, but in the last rays of the sunlight that fell through the leaves of the acers I could still see the lines left by a rake in the fine pebbles at our feet. Stanley, as always, was wearing a somewhat crumpled grey suit and brown suede shoes, and, as always when we talked to each other, he inclined as far as he could toward me with his whole body, not only in order to show his interest but also out of a punctilious courtesy. The leaning posture which he adopted recalled that of a man walking into the wind, or a ski jumper who has launched himself into the air. Talking to Stanley, one not uncommonly had the feeling that he came gliding down from on high. When he was listening, he would tilt his head to one side, smiling blissfully, but when he himself was speaking it was as though he were desperately struggling for breath. Often his face would contort into a grimace, the effort bringing beads of perspiration to his brow, and the words came from him in a spasmodic, precipitate manner that betrayed severe inner turmoil and presaged, even then, that all too soon his heart would cease to beat. When I now think back to Stanley Kerry, it seems incomprehensible that the paths of Michael's life and mine should have intersected in the person of that extraordinarily shy man, and that at the time we met him, in 1944 and in 1966 respectively, we were both twenty-two. No matter how often I tell myself that chance happenings of this kind occur far more often than we suspect, since we all move, one after the other, along the same roads mapped out for us by our origins and our hopes, my rational mind is nonetheless unable to lay the ghosts of repetition that haunt me with ever greater frequency. Scarcely am I in company but it seems as if I had already heard the same opinions expressed by the same people somewhere or other, in the same way, with the same words, turns of phrase and gestures. The physical sensation closest to this feeling of repetition, which sometimes lasts for several minutes and can be quite disconcerting, is that of the peculiar numbness brought on by a heavy loss of blood, often resulting in a temporary inability to think, to speak or to move one's limbs, as though, without being aware of it, one had suffered a stroke. Perhaps there is in this as yet unexplained phenomenon of apparent duplication some kind of anticipation of the end, a venture into the void, a sort of disengagement, which, like a gramophone repeatedly playing the same sequence of notes, has less to do with damage to the machine itself than with an irreparable defect in its programme. Be that as it may, on that August afternoon at Michael's house I felt several times, either through exhaustion or for some other reason, that I was losing the ground from under my feet. When at last the time came for me to take my leave, Anne, who had been resting for an hour or so, entered the room and sat down with us. I cannot remember whether it was she who turned the conversation to the fact that nobody wears mourning any more, not even a black band on the sleeve or a black stud in the lapel. At all events, in that connection she told the story of a certain Mr Squirrel from Middleton who was almost of retirement age and who, as far as anyone knew, had never worn anything but mourning, not even as a young man before he was apprenticed to the undertaker in Westleton. Contrary to what his name suggests, said Anne, Mr Squirrel was not particularly spry or nimble. In fact he was a swarthy, ponderous giant of a man whom the undertaker presumably employed as pallbearer more for his exceptional physical strength than his propensity to mourn. In the village, Anne went on, it was thought that Squirrel had no memory at all, and was quite unable to recall what had happened in his childhood, last year, last month or even last week. How he could therefore grieve for the dead was a puzzle to which no one knew the answer. Another foible of Squirrel's was that, despite his lack of a memory, he had always wanted to be an actor, ever since he was a boy, and had so persistently pestered the people in

Middleton and other nearby villages who occasionally put on a play that in the end, when there was to be an open-air production of *King Lear* on Westleton Heath, he was given the part of the gentleman in the seventh scene of act four who, except for a line or two, remains silent throughout. Squirrel laboured a whole year at learning by heart those few lines, said Anne, which on the night he did indeed deliver most movingly, and to this day he repeats the one or other, whether the occasion suits or not, as I once discovered for myself when I said good morning to him and he replied in sonorous tones across the street: They say Edgar, his banish'd son, is with the Earl of Kent in Germany. Shortly after Anne had finished her story, I asked her to call a taxi for me. When she returned from making the call, she said that, as she replaced the receiver, the dream she had had just before she awoke from her afternoon nap came back to her. We were all three in Norwich, she said, and, because Michael still had appointments to keep, I had ordered a taxi for her. When it drove up it proved to be a large, gleaming limousine. I held the door open for her and she climbed into the back. Without a sound the limousine began to move, and, before she had settled herself, she was out of the town and surrounded by an immense forest, shot through by rays of sunlight, which extended over many miles all the way down to the Middleton house. At an even speed that could neither be said to be fast nor slow we travelled along a soft, gently curving track. The atmosphere through which the car moved was denser than air and somewhat resembled streaming currents of deep, silent water. She saw the forest, Anne said, with absolute clarity and in meticulous detail impossible to put into words, as it slid past outside: the tiny fruit capsules on stems protruding from patches and cushions of moss, the hair-thin grass stalks, the quivering ferns and the upright grey and brown, smooth or rough-barked trunks of trees that were lost a few yards up amidst the impenetrable leafage of the evergreens growing amongst them. Higher still were clusters of mistletoe, mimosa and lobelia, and cascading down into them from the next level of this luxuriant forest realm, in clouds of snow-white or pink, were hundreds of flowering plants and lianas from branches that reached out like the yard arms of great sailing ships, festooned with bromeliads and orchids. And above these, at a height the eye could hardly attain, the tops of palms swayed to and fro, their delicate, feathery, fan-shaped fronds of that unfathomable green which seems underlaid with burnished brass and which Leonardo used for the crowns of his trees, in the *Annunciation*, for instance, or the portrait of Ginevra de Benci. I have only an indistinct notion of how beautiful it all was, said Anne, nor can I properly describe now the feeling of being driven in that limousine that appeared to have no one at the wheel. It was not really like driving at all, it was more like floating, in a way I have not experienced since my childhood, when I was able to hover a few inches above the ground. As Anne was talking, we had walked out together into the garden, where night had already fallen. We waited for the taxi beside the Hölderlin pump, and by the faint light that fell from the living-room window into the well I saw, with a shudder that went to the roots of my hair, a beetle rowing across the surface of the water, from one dark shore to the other.

VIII

The day after my visit to Middleton I fell into conversation with a Dutchman named Cornelis de Jong in the bar of the Crown Hotel in Southwold. He had been to Suffolk on a number of occasions and was now thinking of buying one of the vast properties, often running to more than a thousand hectares, that are regularly offered by estate agents hereabouts. De Jong told me that he had grown up on a sugar plantation near Surabaya and later, after studying at the Wageningen Agricultural College, continued the family tradition in a somewhat straitened fashion as a sugar-beet farmer in the Deventer area. If he was now planning to transfer his interests to England, it was primarily for economic reasons, said de Jong. Single estates of the size regularly appearing on the East Anglian market never came up for sale in Holland, and manor houses of the kind that were practically thrown in for nothing with the land here were not to be found at home either. In their heyday, said de Jong, the Dutch invested chiefly in cities, while the English put their money into country estates. That evening in the bar, we talked till last orders were called about the rise and decline of the two nations and about the curiously close relationship that existed, until well into the twentieth century, between the history of sugar and the history of art. For long periods of time there was little scope for an ostentatious display of accumulated wealth, and consequently the enormous profits that accrued to the few families who grew and traded in sugar cane were largely lavished on the building, furnishing and maintenance of magnificent country residences and stately town houses. It was Cornelis de Jong who drew my attention to the fact that many important museums, such as the Mauritshuis in The Hague or the Tate Gallery in London, were originally endowed by the sugar dynasties or were in some other way connected with the sugar trade. The capital amassed in the eighteenth and nineteenth centuries through various forms of slave economy is still in circulation, said de Jong, still bearing interest, increasing many times over and continually burgeoning anew. One of the most tried and tested ways of legitimizing this kind of money has always been patronage of the arts, the purchase and exhibiting of paintings and sculptures, a practice which today, said de Jong, was leading to a relentless escalation of prices paid at major auctions. Within a few years, the hundred million mark for half a square yard of painted canvas will have been passed. At times it seems to me, said de Jong, as if all works of art were coated with a sugar glaze or indeed made completely of sugar, like the model of the battle of Esztergom created by a confectioner to the Viennese court, which Empress Maria Theresia, so it is said, devoured in one of her recurrent bouts of melancholy. The morning after our conversation in the Crown Hotel Bar,

Grondbewerking.
The tilling of the ground.

which extended to the plantation and production methods employed in the Dutch East Indies, I drove down to Woodbridge with de Jong. The arable land he wanted to view stretched westward from the outskirts of that small town, and was bordered to the north by the deserted estate of Boulge, which I had in any case intended to visit, for it was at Boulge that the writer Edward FitzGerald grew up almost two hundred years ago, and there too he was buried in the summer of 1883. After I had parted from Cornelis de Jong, with a warmth which it seemed he returned, I first crossed the fields from the A12 towards Bredfield, where FitzGerald was born on the 31st of March 1809 at the White House, of which all that now remains is the orangery. The main wing of the building, which went back to the mid-eighteenth century and could accommodate a large family and a no-less numerous staff of servants, was levelled to the ground in May 1944 when one of the German V-bombs, which the English nicknamed "doodlebugs", suddenly deviated from its course and caused wholly pointless damage in remote Bredfield. Boulge Hall, the neighbouring manor house into which the FitzGeralds moved in 1825, has also gone. After it burnt down in 1926, the charred walls long remained standing in the heart of the estate. Not until after the Second World War was the ruin completely demolished, presumably for building material. The park itself is now neglected, and the grass has gone unmown for years. The great oaks are dying branch by branch, and the driveways, patched up here and there with broken bricks, are full of potholes brimming with black water. The copse which encloses the little church of Boulge, which the FitzGeralds restored in a rather infelicitous fashion, is similarly neglected. Rotting timber, rusting iron and other debris lies around everywhere. The graves are half sunk into the ground, overshadowed by the encroaching sycamores. Small wonder, I thought, that FitzGerald, who abhorred funerals and indeed every kind of ceremony, did not wish to be buried in this sombre place and wanted his ashes scattered on the

glittering waters of the sea. If, nonetheless, he lies here, in a grave beside the hideous family mausoleum, it is owing to one of those wicked ironies against which even last wills and testaments are powerless. The FitzGeralds were an old Anglo-Norman family and had lived in Ireland for more than six hundred years before Edward FitzGerald's parents decided to settle in the county of Suffolk. The family fortune, amassed over generations through warring feuds with other lords, by ruthless subjection of the local people and by a no less ruthless marriage strategy, was legendary even at a time when the wealth of the topmost social strata was beginning to exceed all that had hitherto been known, and consisted principally, apart from properties in England, of their vast land holdings in Ireland, together with the goods and chattels, and hosts of peasants who were effectively no more than their serfs. Mary Frances FitzGerald, Edward's mother, was the sole heir to this fortune, and thus without any doubt one of the richest women in the kingdom. Her cousin, John Purcell, whom she had married, mindful of the family's motto "stesso sangue, stessa sorte", gave up his own name in favour of the name of FitzGerald, in recognition of his wife's superior position; while for her part, needless to say, Mary Frances FitzGerald saw to it that her title to the fortune was not diminished in the smallest degree by her marriage to John Purcell. The portraits that have come down to us show her as a formidable woman with powerful, sloping shoulders, a truly awe-inspiring bust, and an overall appearance that astounded many contemporaries by its resemblance to the Duke of Wellington. As one would expect, the cousin she had married soon paled to a negligible if not contemptible figure beside her, especially since none of his attempts to secure for himself a position in the rapidly proliferating new industries met with any success. He tried his hand as a mining entrepreneur and at various other speculative ventures, but one after another failed until at length he had gone through all of his own not inconsiderable fortune as well as the money his wife had made available to him. After bankruptcy proceedings in a London courtroom, all that remained to him was the reputation of being a hopeless and chronic defaulter, kept by the charity of his wife. Hence he spent most of his time at the family seat in Suffolk, hunting quail and snipe and occupying himself in other similar ways, while Mary Frances held court at her London residence. Occasionally she would arrive at Bredfield in a canary-yellow carriage drawn by four black horses, with a luggage waggon and a large number of footmen and lady's maids in her retinue, to see how the children were and to uphold, by a brief sojourn in the house, her claims to dominion in this, from her point of view, impossibly remote place. Whenever she arrived or departed, Edward and his siblings would stand petrified at the windows of their attic nursery or hide in the driveway shrubbery, too intimidated by her splendour to dare run towards her, or wave goodbye. Even when he was past sixty, FitzGerald recalled that on visits to Bredfield his mother would sometimes come upstairs and there, enveloped in her rustling clothes and a great cloud of scent, would stalk to and fro like some strange giantess for a while, remarking upon this or that, only to disappear once again down the steep staircase, leaving us children, as he said, not much comforted. Since their father was increasingly absorbed in his own world, the young FitzGeralds were left entirely in the care of their nanny and tutor, whose rooms were also on the top floor and who tended to take out on their charges their suppressed rage at the disrespect many a time shown them by their masters. The fear of these reprisals and the humiliation that went with them hung over the children's daily routine which, apart from the cheerless meals they had to take with their minders, was governed by eternal arithmetic and writing exercises, the most odious of which was penning a weekly report to Mother. In addition to this regime, they suffered from extreme boredom, for they had next to no contact with others their own age and thus all they could think of doing in their free time was to lie day-dreaming for hours on the blue-varnished floorboards in the nursery or to gaze out of the windows into the park, where hardly a living soul was ever to be seen. At best the gardener would be pushing a wheelbarrow across the lawn or Father would be returning from a shoot with the gamekeeper. Only on rare crystal-clear days, FitzGerald later recalled, could one sometimes see beyond Bredfield and indistinctly discern, over the tree tops, the white sails of ships off the coast ten miles away; and then one would lose oneself in vague dreams of liberation from this childhood dungeon. Later, when he had finished his studies at Cambridge, FitzGerald's horror of his heavily-carpeted family home stuffed with gilded furniture, works of art, and trophies of travel was so great that he refused to set foot in it again. Instead of taking up residence there, in keeping with his station, he moved into a tiny two-roomed cottage on the perimeter of the estate, and there he spent the next fifteen years, from 1837 till 1853, leading a bachelor life that in many respects anticipated his later eccentricity. In the main he kept himself occupied in his hermitage with reading, in a variety of languages, with writing countless letters, with making notes towards a dictionary of commonplaces, with compiling a complete glossary of all words and phrases relating to the sea and to seafaring and with pasting up scrap books of every conceivable description. He had a particular predilection for the correspondence of bygone ages, such as that of Madame de Sévigné, who became far more real to him than even his friends who were still alive. Time after time he read what she had written, quoted her in his own letters, continuously added to the materials he was assembling for a Sévigné dictionary which would not only provide commentary on all her correspondents and all the persons and places referred to in their exchanges but would also offer a key of sorts to the way in which she had cultivated and developed the art of writing. FitzGerald did not complete the Sévigné project any more than he completed his other literary schemes, and probably never wanted to. It was not until 1914, when the era came to a close, that one of his great-nieces edited two tomes, now extremely hard to come by, from that voluminous compilation, which lies preserved in a few cardboard boxes in Trinity College library. The only task FitzGerald finished and published in his lifetime was his marvellous rendering of the *Rubaiyat* of the Persian poet Omar Khayyam, with whom he felt a curiously close affinity across a distance of eight centuries. FitzGerald described the endless hours he spent translating this poem of two hundred and twenty-four lines as a colloquy with the dead man and an attempt to bring to us tidings of him. The English verses he devised for the purpose, which radiate with a pure, seemingly unselfconscious beauty, feign an anonymity that disdains even the least claim to authorship, and draw us, word by word, to an invisible point where the mediaeval orient and the fading occident can come together in a way never allowed them by the calamitous course of history. *For in and out, above, about, below, / 'Tis nothing but a Magic Shadow-Show, /*

Play'd in a Box whose Candle is the Sun, / Round which the Phantom Figures come and go. The *Rubaiyat* was published in 1859, and it was also in that year that William Browne, who probably meant more to FitzGerald than anyone else on earth, died a painful death from serious injuries sustained in a hunting accident. The paths of the two men had first crossed on a walking tour of Wales, when FitzGerald was twenty-three and Browne just sixteen. In a letter written immediately after Browne's death, FitzGerald recalled how deeply moved he had been when, on the morning after he had conversed for a while with Browne on the steamer from Bristol, he met him again in the Tenby boarding house where they had both taken quarters and how Browne, with a chalk mark from playing billiards on his face, had seemed to him then like someone he had missed for goodness knew how long. In the years that followed that first meeting in Wales, Browne and FitzGerald often visited each other in Suffolk or Bedfordshire, driving cross-country in a gig or rambling over the fields, lunching at inns, watching the clouds as they drifted eastward, and perhaps feeling the wing of time brush their temples. A little riding, driving, eating, drinking etc. (not forgetting smoke) fill up the day, FitzGerald wrote. Browne would have his fishing rods with him, his shotgun, and watercolour requisites, whilst FitzGerald would take a book which he scarcely read because he could not take his eyes off his friend. We do not know whether he allowed himself, then or at any other time, to ponder the nature of the desire that moved him, but his constant anxiety for Browne's health was in itself indicative of the depth of his passion. For FitzGerald, Browne was the personification of an ideal, but for that very reason he seemed overshadowed by mortality from the start, and prompted fears in FitzGerald that perhaps he will not be long to be looked at. For there are signs of decay about him. Browne's subsequent marriage did not change the feelings FitzGerald had for him in the slightest, but instead confirmed his obscure intuition that he would not be able to keep him and that his friend was destined for an early death. The love which FitzGerald probably never dared to declare was not expressed until he wrote his letter of condolence to Browne's widow, who doubtless laid his curious communication aside in amazement if not consternation. FitzGerald was in his fiftieth year when he lost Browne. From then on he withdrew increasingly within himself. He had long been refusing his mother's regular invitations to her sumptuous dinner parties in London, because to his mind the ritual of communal dining was the most abominable of Society's abominations, and now he also forwent his occasional visits to the capital's galleries and concert halls, only in exceptional instances venturing beyond his immediate circle of friends. I think I shall shut myself up in the remotest nook of Suffolk and let my beard grow, he wrote, and would doubtless have done just that, had he not become disaffected with that region too, where a new breed of landowners were working the soil for all it could yield. They are felling all the trees, he complained, and tearing up the hedgerows. Soon the birds will not know where to go. One copse after another is vanishing, the grassy wayside banks where in the spring the cowslips and violets bloomed have been ploughed up and levelled, and if one now takes the path from Bredfield to Hasketon, which was once so delightful, it is like crossing a desert. Given the aversion that FitzGerald had had since childhood to his own class, the ruthless exploitation of the land, the obsession with private property, which was pursued by means increasingly dubious, and the ever more radical restriction of common rights, were profoundly abhorrent to him. And so, he said, I get to the water: where no friends are buried nor Pathways stopt up. From 1860, FitzGerald

spent a large part of his time either by the sea or on board the ocean-going yacht he had had built and named Scandal. From Woodbridge he would sail down the Deben and up the coast to Lowestoft, where he hired his crew from among the herring fishers, all the time looking for a face that reminded him of William Browne. FitzGerald sailed far out into the German Ocean, and, just as he had always refused to dress for particular occasions, so, insteading of donning one of the newly fashionable yachting outfits, he would wear an old frock coat and a top hat tied fast. The sole concession he made to the stylish appearance expected of a yachtsman was the long white feather boa which he reportedly liked to sport on deck and which fluttered behind him in the breeze, visible at a good distance. In the late summer of 1863, FitzGerald decided to cross to Holland in the Scandal in order to see the portrait of the young Louis Trip, painted by Ferdinand Bol in 1652, which was in the museum in The Hague. Upon arrival in Rotterdam, his travelling companion, one George Manby of Woodbridge, persuaded him to view the great seaport first. Consequently, wrote FitzGerald, the two of us went about all day long in an open carriage, now this way, now that, till I no longer had any idea where I was, and that evening I fell exhausted into my bed. The following day passed in Amsterdam in a like unpleasant fashion, and not until the third day did we finally arrive in The Hague, after all manner of tedious incidents, only to find the museum closing until the beginning of the next week. FitzGerald, his patience already sorely tried by the irritations of travel on land, interpreted this incomprehensible exclusion as a mean trick the Dutch were playing on him personally, threw a fearful fit of rage and despair in which he variously berated the narrow-minded Dutch, his companion George Manby and himself, and insisted on returning to Rotterdam forthwith and setting sail for home. – In those years, FitzGerald spent the winter months in Woodbridge, where he had lodgings at a gunsmith's on Market Hill. Often he was to be seen walking about the town lost in thought, wearing his Inverness cape and usually, even in bad weather, only slippers on his feet. Behind him followed his black labrador, Bletsoe, which had been a gift from Browne. In 1869, after a dispute with the gunsmith's wife, who found her lodger's eccentric ways unacceptable, FitzGerald moved into his last home, a somewhat dilapidated farmhouse on the outskirts of Woodbridge, and there, as he put it, he settled to await the final act. His requirements, always modest in the extreme, had become even fewer in the course of time. For decades he had eaten a diet of vegetables, offended as he was by the consumption of large quantities of rare meat which his contemporaries considered necessary to keep one's strength up, and now he altogether dispensed with the chore of cooking, which struck him as absurd, and took little but bread, butter and tea. On fine days he sat in the garden surrounded by doves, and at other times often spent long periods at the window, which afforded a view of a goose green fringed by pollarded trees. In this solitude, as his letters show, he continued in remarkably good cheer, even though he was at times assailed by what he called the blue devil of melancholy, which had been the undoing years before of his beautiful sister Andalusia. In the autumn of 1877 he went to London once more, to see a performance of *The Magic Flute*. At the last moment, however, he was so dispirited by the November fog, the wet, and the dirt in the streets, that he decided against the planned visit to Covent Garden, which, he wrote, would doubtless only have spoiled the memories of Malibran and Sontag so dear to him. I think it is now best, he wrote, to attend these Operas as given in the Theatre of one's own Recollections. But there was to be little time for FitzGerald to stage such performances in his mind, for the imaginary music was drowned out by the tinnitus that troubled him now. Moreover, his eyesight grew steadily weaker. He was obliged to wear spectacles with blue- or green-tinted lenses, and had his housekeeper's boy read to him. A photograph from the 1870s, the only one he ever had taken, shows him with head averted because (he wrote

apologetically to his nieces) his ailing eyes blinked too much if he looked directly into the camera. – Every summer, FitzGerald paid a visit of a few days to his friend George Crabbe, who was vicar of Merton in Norfolk. In June 1883 he made the journey for the last time. Merton is no further than sixty miles from Woodbridge, but travelling there over the meandering railway network that had spread everywhere during FitzGerald's lifetime involved five changes and took a whole day. What was stirring within FitzGerald's breast as he leant back in his carriage watching the hedgerows and cornfields pass by outside is not recorded, but perhaps it resembled the feelings he once experienced as he sat in the mail coach from Leicester to Cambridge, when the sight of the summer countryside made him feel like an angel because suddenly, without knowing why, he found he had tears of happiness in his eyes. At Merton, Crabbe met him from the train in his dog cart. It had been a long and especially hot day, but FitzGerald remarked on the cool air and remained wrapped tight in his plaid as they drove. At table he drank a little tea but declined to eat anything. Around nine he asked for a glass of brandy and water and retired upstairs to bed. Early next morning, Crabbe heard him moving about his room, but when he went somewhat later to summon him to breakfast he found him stretched out on his bed and no longer among the living.

The shadows were lengthening as I walked in from Boulge Park to Woodbridge, where I put up for the night at the Bull Inn. The room to which I was shown by the landlord was under the roof. The clinking of glasses in the bar and a low murmur of talk rose up the staircase, with the occasional exclamation or laugh. After time was called, things gradually quietened down. I heard the woodwork of the old half-timber building, which had expanded in the heat of the day and was now contracting fraction by fraction, creaking and groaning. In the gloom of the unfamiliar room, my eyes involuntarily turned in the direction from which the sounds came, looking for the crack that might run along the low ceiling, the spot where the plaster was flaking from the wall or the mortar crumbling behind the panelling. And if I closed my eyes for a while it felt as if I were in a cabin aboard a ship on the high seas, as if the whole building were rising on the swell of a wave, shuddering a little on the crest, and then, with a sigh, subsiding into the depths. I did not get to sleep until day was breaking and the song of a blackbird was in my ear, and shortly thereafter I awoke once more from a dream in which I beheld FitzGerald, my companion of the day before, sitting at a little blue metal table in his garden in his shirtsleeves and wearing a black silk jabot and a tall top hat. Hollyhocks grown higher than a man were flowering around him, chickens were scratching about in a sandy hollow under an elder tree, and his black dog, Bletsoe, lay stretched out in the shade, whilst I, though in the dream I was unable to see myself and was thus like a ghost, sat opposite FitzGerald, playing a game of dominoes with him. Beyond the flower garden an even green park, utterly deserted, extended to the very edge of the world, where the minarets of Khorasan soared. It was not, however, the park of the FitzGerald estate at Boulge, but that of a country house at the foot of the Slieve Bloom Mountains in Ireland where I had been a guest for a short time some years ago. In my dream I could make out far off in the distance the three-storey ivy-covered house where the Ashburys presumably still lead their secluded lives to this day; at least, it was a very secluded and indeed quite bizarre life at the time when I met them. Coming from the mountains, I had enquired after accommodation in a small, gloomy shop in Clarahill. I remember that the proprietor, a Mr O'Hare, who was wearing a curious cinnamon-coloured overcoat of thin calico, involved me in a lengthy conversation concerning Newton's theory of gravity. At some point in this talk, Mr O'Hare suddenly interrupted himself and exclaimed: The Ashburys might put you up. One of the daughters came in here some years ago with a note offering Bed and Breakfast. I was supposed to display it in the shop window. I can't think what became of it or whether they ever had any guests. Perhaps I removed it when the letters had paled in the sun. Or perhaps they came and removed it themselves. Mr O'Hare then drove me to the Ashburys in his delivery van and waited on the weedy forecourt until I was asked in. I had to knock several times before the door was opened and Catherine stood there in her faded red summer dress, with an odd stiffness that suggested she had been arrested in mid-movement by the sight of this unannounced stranger. She gazed at me wide-eyed, or rather, she looked right through me. Once I had explained why I was there, it took some time for her to recover her composure, to step a pace aside, and gesture with her left hand, scarcely perceptibly, for me to come in and take a seat in the hall. As she walked away across the stone flags, in silence, I noticed that she was barefoot. Without a sound she vanished in the darkness of the background, and just as soundlessly reappeared a few minutes later, to escort me up a staircase the broad steps of which made climbing astonishingly easy, to the first floor and along various passages to a large room, where the high windows afforded a view over the roofs of the stables and outhouses and the kitchen garden onto haymeadows combed by the wind. Beyond there were trees in various shades of green and, above them, the faint line of the mountains, barely distinguishable from the even blue of the sky. I cannot say how long I stood by one of the three windows, engrossed in that view; all I remember is hearing Catherine, who was waiting in the doorway, say, Will this be all right? and that, as I turned to her, I stammered some incoherent reply. Only when Catherine had gone did I take in the full size of the room. The floorboards were covered with a velvety layer of dust. The curtains had gone and the paper had been stripped off the walls, which had traces of whitewash with bluish streaks like the skin of a dying body, and reminded me of one of those maps of the far north on which next to nothing is marked. The only items of furniture in the room were a table and chair and a narrow collapsible iron bedstead of the kind that army officers used to have with them on campaigns. Whenever I rested on that bed over the next few days, my consciousness began to dissolve at the edges, so that at times I could hardly have said how I had got there or indeed where I was. Repeatedly I felt as if I were lying in a traumatic fever in some kind of field hospital. From outside I heard the cries of the peacocks, which went right through me, but what I saw in my mind's eye was not the yard in which they perched on the very top of the junk that had been piling up there for years but a battlefield somewhere in Lombardy over which the vultures circled, and, all around, a country laid waste by war. The armies had long since marched on. I alone, falling from one swoon into the next, was left in a house that had been looted of everything. These images became the more real in my head because the Ashburys lived under their roof like refugees who have come through dreadful ordeals and do not now dare to settle in the place where they have ended up. It struck me that all the members of the family were continually wandering hither and thither along the corridors and up and down the stairs. One rarely saw them sitting calm and collected, singly or together. Even their meals they usually ate standing. What work they did always had about it something aimless and meaningless and seemed not so much part of a daily routine as an expression of a deeply engrained distress. Ever since leaving school in 1974, Edmund, the youngest, had been working on a fat-bellied boat a good ten yards in length, although, as he casually informed me, he knew nothing about boat-building and had no intention of ever going to sea in his unshapely barge. It's not going to be launched. It's just something I do. I have to have something to do. Mrs Ashbury collected flower seeds in paper bags. Once she had written the name, date, location, colour and other details on the bags, she would clap them over the dead heads of the blooms, in the overgrown flower beds or further afield in the meadows, and tie them up with string. Then she would cut off the stalks, bring the bagged heads indoors and hang them up on a much-knotted line that criss-crossed what was once the library. There were so many of these white-bagged flower-stalks hanging under the library ceiling that they resembled clouds of paper, and when Mrs Ashbury stood on the library steps to hang up or take down the rustling seed-bags she half-vanished among them like a saint ascending into heaven. Once they had been taken down, the bags were stored under some inscrutable system on the shelves, which had evidently long since been unburdened of books. I do not think Mrs Ashbury had any idea what distant fields the seeds she collected might one day fall on, any more than Catherine and her two sisters Clarissa and Christina knew why they spent several hours every day in one of the north-facing rooms, where they had stored great quantities of remnant fabrics, sewing multi-coloured pillowcases, counterpanes and similar items. Like giant children under an evil spell, the three unmarried daughters, much of an age, sat on the floor amidst these mountains of material, working away and only rarely breathing a word to each other. The movement they made as they drew the thread sideways and upwards with every stitch reminded me of things that were so far back in the past that I felt my heart sink at the thought of how little time now remained. On one occasion Clarissa told me that she and her sisters had once intended to start an interior decorating business, but the plan came to nothing, she said, both because of their inexperience and because there was no call in their neighbourhood for such a service. Perhaps that was why they mostly undid what they had sewn either on the same day, the next day or the day after that. It was also possible that in their imagination they envisaged something of such extraordinary beauty that the work they completed invariably disappointed them. At least that was what I thought, when on one of my visits to their workshop they showed me the pieces that had been spared the unstitching. One of them, a bridal gown made of hundreds of scraps of silk embroidered with silken thread, or rather woven over cobweb-fashion, which hung on a headless tailor's dummy, was a work of art so colourful and of such intricacy and perfection that it seemed almost to have come to life, and at the time I could no more believe my eyes than now I can trust my memory.

On the evening before my departure I was standing out on the terrace with Edmund, leaning on the stone balustrade. It was so quiet that I thought I could hear the cries of the bats that flitted zigzag through the airspace. The park was sinking into darkness when Edmund, after a protracted silence, suddenly said: I have set up the projector in the library. Mother was wondering whether you might want to see what things used to be like here. Inside, Mrs Ashbury was already waiting for the show to begin. I sat down beside her under the paper-bag heavens, the light went out, the projector began to whirr, and on the bare wall above the mantelpiece the mute images of the past appeared, at times quite still and then again following jerkily one upon another, headlong, and rendered unclear by the projection scratches. From a window on the upper floor one looked across the surrounding land, the clumps of trees, fields and meadows, and vice versa, approaching the forecourt from the park, one saw the front of the house, first seeming toy-sized from a distance, then towering ever higher till at length it almost toppled out of the frame. Nowhere was there a sign of neglect. The drive was sanded, the hedges were clipped, the beds in the kitchen garden trim, and the now tumbledown outhouses still well maintained. Later one saw the Ashburys at tea, sitting in a kind of marquee one bright summer's day. It was Edmund's christening, said Mrs Ashbury. Clarissa and Christina were playing badminton. Catherine held a black Scots terrier in her arms. In the background, an old butler was making for the entrance with a laden tray. A maidservant with a cap on her head appeared in the doorway, holding up a hand to shield her eyes from the sun. Edmund put in another reel. Much of what followed had to do with work in the garden and on the estate. I remember a slight lad pushing a huge old-fashioned wheelbarrow; a mower pulled by a tiny pony and steered by a dwarfish driver, mowing straight lines up and down the lawn; a view of a dark hothouse where cucumbers were growing; and a series of over-exposed pictures of a field that looked almost snow-white, where dozens of farm labourers were busy cutting the wheat and binding the sheaves. When the last reel was through there was silence for a long time in the library, which was now lit only dimly by the light from the hall. Not until Edmund had stowed the projector in its case and left the room did Mrs Ashbury begin to speak. She told me that she had married in 1946, immediately after her husband came out of the army, and that a few months later, following the sudden death of her father-in-law, they had come to Ireland, quite contrary to the expectations both of them had of their future life, to take possession of the property he had inherited, which was then as good as unsaleable. At that time, said Mrs Ashbury, she had had not the slightest notion of Ireland's Troubles, and to this day they remained alien to her. I remember waking the first night in this house, feeling I was completely out of this world. The moon was shining in at the window, and the light lay so strangely on the layer of wax left on the floor by more than a century of dripping candles that I felt I was adrift on a sea of quicksilver. My husband, said Mrs Ashbury, never said a word about the Troubles, on principle, although he must have witnessed terrible things during the civil war, or perhaps because of that. Only little by little, from the curt answers he gave to my questions on the matter, did I piece together something of his family history, and the history of the land-owning class that became hopelessly impoverished in the decades following the civil war. But the picture I put together was never more than a rough sketch. Apart from my extremely reticent husband, said Mrs Ashbury, my only other source of information was the legends about the Troubles, part tragic and part ludicrous, that had formed during the long years of decline in the heads of our servants, whom we had inherited together with the rest of the inventory and who were themselves already part of history, as it were. Years after we moved in, for instance, I learnt a little from our butler, Quincey, about that dreadful midsummer night in 1920 when the Randolphs' house six miles away was set on fire while the Randolphs themselves were dining with my future parents-in-law. According to Quincey, the rebel Republicans first assembled the servants in the hall and told them without further ado that they had one hour to pack their personal belongings and make some tea for themselves and the freedom fighters, and then a great fire of retribution would be raised. First, said Mrs Ashbury, the children were woken, and the dogs and cats, which were quite beside themselves with premonitions of disaster, were rounded up. Later, according to Quincey, who was Colonel Randolph's valet at the time, all the inhabitants of the house stood out on the lawn amongst items of luggage and furniture and all the nonsensical things one grabs at in a state of panic and fear. At the last moment, in Quincey's telling, he had had to run up to the second floor one more time to rescue the cockatiel that belonged to old Mrs Randolph, who, as it turned out on the following day, was deprived in the catastrophe of her up until then perfectly lucid mind. Powerless, they were all forced to stand by as the Republicans dragged a big drum of petrol from the garage across the courtyard and then, with a loud Heave ho!, rolled it up the steps and into the hall, where they spilled out the contents. Within minutes of the first torch being hurled in, the flames were shooting from the windows and the roof, and before long it was as if one was looking into an immense furnace full of red-hot fire and flying sparks. I do not think, said Mrs Ashbury, that one can even begin to imagine the thoughts of the victims when they witness a sight like that. At all events, the Randolphs, who had always lived fearing the worst and yet did not believe that it could ever happen, were alerted by a gardener who had escaped on a bicycle, and, accompanied by my parents-in-law, drove over to the blaze, which was visible from a long way off. When they arrived at the scene of destruction, those who had started the fire had long disappeared, and all they could do was hug their children and join those huddled together there speechless and paralysed with horror like shipwrecked survivors on a raft. Not till daybreak did the fire abate and the black contours of the burnt-out shell stand out against the sky. The ruin, said Mrs Ashbury, was subsequently demolished. That was before my time, and I never saw it. They say two or three hundred country houses were burnt down during the civil war, regardless of whether they were relatively modest properties or stately homes such as

Summerhill, where the Austrian Empress Elisabeth had once been so happy. To the best of my knowledge, said Mrs Ashbury, people were never harmed by the rebels. Evidently burning the houses down was the most effective way of driving out those families who were identified, rightly or wrongly, with the detested rule of the English. In the years after the end of the civil war, even those who had survived unscathed left the country if they possibly could. The only ones who stayed on were those who had no livelihood except what they derived from their estates. Every attempt to sell the houses and land was doomed to failure from the very start, because in the first place there were no buyers far and wide, and in the second, even if a purchaser had appeared, one could hardly have lived in Bournemouth or Kensington for more than a month on the proceeds. At the same time, nobody in Ireland had any idea how they could possibly go on. Farming was in the doldrums, labourers were demanding wages nobody could afford to pay, fewer crops were being planted, and incomes were steadily diminishing. The situation grew more hopeless with every year, and the signs of increasing poverty, apparent everywhere, grew more and more ominous. Keeping up the houses even in the most rudimentary way had long been impossible. The paintwork was flaking off the window encasements and the doors; the curtains became threadbare; the wallpaper peeled off the walls; the upholstery was worn out; it was raining in everywhere, and people put out tin tubs, bowls and pots to catch the water. Soon they were obliged to abandon the rooms on the upper storeys, or even whole wings, and retreat to more or less usable quarters on the ground floor. The window panes in the locked-up rooms misted over with cobwebs, dry rot advanced, vermin bore the spores of mould to every nook and cranny, and monstrous brownish-purple and black fungal growths appeared on the walls and ceilings, often the size of an ox-head. The floorboards began to give, the beams of the ceilings sagged, and the panelling and staircases, long since rotten within, crumbled to sulphurous yellow dust, at times overnight. Every so often, usually after a long period of rain or extended droughts or indeed after any change in the weather, a sudden, disastrous collapse would occur in the midst of the encroaching decay that went almost unnoticed, and had assumed the character of normality. Just as people supposed they could hold a particular line, some dramatic and unanticipated deterioration would compel them to evacuate further areas, till they really had no way out and found themselves forced to the last post, prisoners in their own homes. They say that a great-uncle of my husband's in County Clare, who used to run his house in the grand style, ended up living in the kitchen, said Mrs Ashbury. For years all he supposedly ate for dinner was a simple dish of poatoes prepared by his butler, who now had to double as his cook, though he did still wear a black dinner jacket and open a bottle of Bordeaux, the cellar not being quite empty yet. Great-uncle and the butler, who were both called William, so Quincey told me, and died on the same day, both well past the age of eighty, had their beds in the kitchen, said Mrs Ashbury, and goodness knows how often I have wondered whether it was a sense of duty that kept the butler going till his master no longer needed him, or whether great-uncle gave up the ghost when his exhausted servant passed away, knowing that without his presence he wouldn't survive a single day. Probably it was the servants, who often worked for decades for scant wages and were no more able to find a place elsewhere at so advanced an age than their masters were, who kept things more or less ticking over. When they lay down to die, the end of those they had looked after was often imminent as well. In our own case it was no different, except that we shared in the general decline rather late in the day. I soon realized that if the Ashburys had been able to keep their property until after the War, it was purely because they kept putting in money from a substantial legacy left to them in the early Thirties, which had shrunk to a tiny amount by the time my husband died. Even so, I was always convinced that things would improve one day. I simply refused to believe that the society we were part of had long since collapsed. Shortly after we arrived in Ireland, Gormanston Castle was sold at auction. Straffan was sold in 1949, Cartin in 1950, French Park in 1953, Killeen Rockingham in 1957, Powerscourt in 1961, not to mention the smaller estates. The extent of our family fiasco only became clear to me when I had to fend for myself and try to support us all somehow. Since I had no money to pay the labourers' wages, I soon had no choice but to give up farming. We sold off the land bit by bit, which kept the worst at bay for a few years, and as long as we had one or two servants in the house it was still possible to keep up appearances, to the outside world and in our own eyes. When Quincey died, I no longer knew what to do. First I sold the silver and china at auction, and then little by little the pictures, the books and the furniture. But nobody ever showed an interest in taking on the house, which was getting more and more run down, and so we have remained tied to it, like damned souls to their place. Whatever we have tried, from the girls' sewing to the nursery garden Edmund once started to our notion of having paying guests, has without fail gone wrong. You, said Mrs Ashbury, are the first guest who's ever found his way here in the almost ten years since we put the advertisement in the Clarahill grocer's window. Unfortunately I am a completely impractical person, caught up in endless trains of thought. All of us are fantasists, ill-equipped for life, the children as much as myself. It seems to me sometimes that we never got used to being on this earth and life is just one great, ongoing, incomprehensible blunder. When Mrs Ashbury had finished her story, I felt that its significance for me lay in an unspoken invitation to stay there with them and share in a life that was becoming more innocent with every day that passed. The fact that I did not do so was a . . . failure that still sometimes seems like a shadow crossing my soul. The next morning, when I came to say goodbye, I had to look for Catherine for a long while. At last I found her in the kitchen garden, which was overgrown with deadly nightshade, valerian, angelica and shot rhubarb. In the red summer frock she was wearing on the day of my arrival, she was leaning against the trunk of the mulberry tree that had once marked the centre of the neatly laid-out herb and vegetable beds within the high brick wall. I made my way through the wilderness to the island of shade from which Catherine was gazing at me. I have come to say goodbye, I said, stepping into the bower formed by the spreading branches. She was holding a broad-brimmed hat like a pilgrim's, the same red as her dress, and now that I was standing beside her she seemed very far away. She looked right through me, her eyes vacant. I have left my address and telephone number, so that if you ever want . . . I broke the sentence off, not knowing how it might continue. In any case, I noticed that Catherine was not listening. At one point, she said after a while, at one point we thought we might raise silkworms in one of the empty rooms, But then we never did. Oh, for the countless things one fails to do! – Years after that last exchange with Catherine Ashbury, I saw her again, or thought I did, in Berlin in March 1993. I had taken the underground to Schlesisches Tor, and after strolling around that dreary part of the city for a time I came upon a small group of people waiting to be admitted to a dilapidated building that might once have been a garage for hackney cabs or something of the kind. According to a billboard, an unfinished play I had never heard of, by Jakob Michael Reinhold Lenz, was to be performed on a stage behind this quite untheatrical façade. In the gloomy space within, the seating proved to be tiny wooden stools, which immediately put one in a childlike mood of craving marvels. Before I could account to myself for my thoughts, there she stood on the stage, incredibly wearing the same red dress, with the same light-coloured hair and holding in her hand the same pilgrim's hat, she or her very image, Catherine of Siena, in an empty room, and then far from her father's house, wearied by the heat of the day and the thorns and stones. In the background, I recall, was a pale view of mountains, perhaps in the Trentino, watery green as if they had just risen from ice-bound polar seas. And Catherine, as the sunlight faded, sank down below a tree, took off her shoes and laid her hat aside. I think I shall sleep here, she said, or rest a little.

Be still, my heart. The tranquil evening will draw its mantle over our ailing senses . . .

From Woodbridge to Orford, down to the sea, is a good four-hour walk. The roads and tracks pass through dry, empty stretches of land which, by the end of a long summer, are almost like a desert. This sparsely populated part of the country has hardly ever been cultivated, and, throughout the ages, was never more than a pasture for sheep reaching from one horizon to the other. When the shepherds and their flocks disappeared in the early nineteenth century, heather and scrub began to spread. This was encouraged as far as possible by the lords of the manors of Rendlesham Hall, Sudbourne Hall, Orwell Park and Ash High House, who had in their possession almost the whole of the Sandlings, in order to create favourable conditions for the hunting of small game, which had become fashionable in the Victorian age. Men of middle-class background who had achieved great wealth through industrial enterprise, wanting to establish a legitimate position in higher society, acquired large country mansions and estates, where they abandoned the utilitarian principles they had always upheld in favour of hunting and shooting, which, although it was quite useless and bent only on destruction, was not considered by anyone as an aberration. In the past, hunting had been the privilege of royalty and the aristocracy, and had been pursued in parks and chases established over centuries especially for the purpose, but now anyone who wanted to transmute their stock market gains into status and repute would hold hunting parties at their estates, several times a season, with as much ostentation as possible. Beside the name and rank of the invited guests, the respect that accrued to the host of such parties was in direct proportion to the number of creatures that were killed. The management of the estate was thus governed by considerations of what was necessary to maintain and increase the stocks of game. Thousands and thousands of pheasants were raised every year in pens, to be let loose later into the huge hunting preserves, which were now lost to farming and made inaccessible. As their rights were curtailed, the rural population not engaged in rearing pheasants, breeding gun dogs, as gamekeepers or beaters or in any other capacity connected with shooting, were forced to quit the places where they had lived for generations. As a consequence, in the early years of the twentieth century, at Hollesley Bay, just inland from the coast, a labour colony later known as Colonial College was established, from which those for whom there was no future went out to New Zealand or Australia after a given time. The Hollesley Bay premises are now a borstal, and young offenders can be seen at work in the fields nearby, always in groups and wearing luminous orange jackets.The pheasant craze was at its height in the decades before the First World War, when Sudbourne Hall alone employed two dozen gamekeepers, and a tailor for the sole purpose of keeping their livery in trim. There were times when six thousand pheasants were gunned down in a single day, not to mention the other fowl, hares and rabbits. The staggering scores were punctiliously recorded in the game books of the rivalling estates. One of the foremost shooting domains in the Sandlings was Bawdsey, with more than eight thousand acres on the north bank of the Deben. In the early 1880s, Sir Cuthbert Quilter, a business baron who had risen from the lower classes, had a family

seat built on a prominent site by the river estuary, reminiscent both of an Elizabethan mansion and of a maharajah's palace. Erecting this architectural marvel was a demonstration for Quilter of the justice of his claim to status, a demonstration quite as unyielding as the choice of his heraldic motto, plutôt mourir que changer, which refuted all bourgeois compromise. At that time, the craving for power in men of his kind was at its most acute. From where they stood there seemed no reason why things should not go on in this vein forever, from one spectacular success to the next. It was no coincidence that the German Empress was taking a convalescent holiday across the river in Felixstowe, which had become a desirable resort in recent years. For weeks, the royal yacht Hohenzollern lay at anchor there, a visible token of the possibilities now open to the entrepreneurial spirit. Under the patronage of their imperial majesties, the North Sea coast might become one great health resort for the upper classes, equipped with all the amenities of modern life. Everywhere, hotels mushroomed from the barren land. Promenades and bathing facilities were established, and piers grew out

into the sea. Even in the most abandoned spot in the entire region, Shingle Street, which now consists of just one wretched row of humble houses and cottages and where I have never encountered a single human being, a spa centre by the grandiose name of German Ocean Mansions designed for two hundred guests was built at the time, if one can believe the records, and staffed with personnel who were recruited from Germany. Today there is no trace of it. Indeed, there seem to have been all manner of ties across the North Sea between the British and German Empires at that period, ties that were expressed first and foremost in the colossal manifestations of bad taste of those who wanted a place in the sun no matter at what cost. Cuthbert Quilter's Anglo-Indian fairy-tale palace in the dunes would doubtless have appealed to the German Kaiser's artistic sensibility, since he had a pronounced penchant for any kind of extravagance. Likewise one can picture Quilter, who added another tower to his beachfront castle for every million he added to his fortune, as a guest aboard the Hohenzollern. One imagines him, say, together with gentlemen from the Admiralty who had also been invited, at the gymnastic exercises which preceded Sunday service at sea. What daring plans might not a man of Quilter's ilk have evolved, egged on by a like-minded man such as Kaiser Wilhelm – envisaging an open-air paradise extending from Felixstowe via Norderney to Sylt, to keep the nations fit; or the foundation of a new North Sea civilization, if not indeed an Anglo-German global alliance, symbolized by a state cathedral, visible far and wide across the waves, on the island of Heligoland. In reality, of course, history took a quite different turn, for, whenever one is imagining a bright future, the next disaster is just around the corner. War was declared, the German hotel employees were sent back home, there were no more summer visitors, and one morning a zeppelin like an airborne whale appeared over the coast, while across the Channel train after train with troops and equipment rolled to the front, whole tracts of land were ploughed up by mortar fire, and the death strip between the front lines was strewn with phosphorescent corpses. The German Kaiser lost his Empire, and the world of Cuthbert Quilter too went into a gradual decline. His means, which had once seemed inexhaustible, dwindled to such an extent that maintaining the estate no longer made any sense. Raymond Quilter, who inherited Bawdsey, entertained the holidaymakers at Felixstowe, who were now of a somewhat less superior breed, with sensational parachute jumps onto the beach. In 1936 he was obliged to sell Bawdsey

Manor to the nation. The proceeds were sufficient to cover his tax liabilities and to finance his passion for flying, which meant more to him than anything else. Having surrendered the family property, he moved into the former chauffeur's quarters, but would still stay at the Dorchester when in London. As a token of the special esteem in which he was held there, the Quilter standard, a golden pheasant on a black ground, was hoisted alongside the Union Jack whenever he arrived. He was accorded this rare privilege by the establishment's reserved staff because of the reputation for chivalry he had enjoyed ever since he had parted, without regret, from the estates his great-uncle had acquired, since which time, apart from a modest amount of independent capital, he had owned nothing but his aeroplane and a runway in an isolated field.

In the years following the First World War, countless estates were broken up in the same way as Quilter's Bawdsey. The manor houses were either left to fall down or used for other purposes, as boys' boarding schools, approved schools, insane asylums, old people's homes, or reception camps for refugees from the Third Reich. Bawdsey Manor itself was for a long time the domicile and research centre of the team under Robert Watson-Watt that developed radar, which now spreads its invisible net throughout the entire airspace. To this day, the area between Woodbridge and the sea remains full of military installations. Time and again, as one walks across the wide plains, one passes barracks, gateways and fenced-off areas where, behind thin plantations of Scots pines, weapons are concealed in camouflaged hangars and grass-covered bunkers, the weapons with which, if an emergency should arise, whole countries and continents can be transformed into smoking heaps of stone and ash in no time. Not far from Orford, and already tired from my long walk, this notion took possession of me when I was hit by a sandstorm. I was approaching the eastern fringe of Rendlesham Forest, which covers several square miles and was for the most part reduced to broken and splintered timber in the terrible hurricane of the 16th of October 1987. Suddenly, in the space of a few minutes, the bright sky darkened and a wind came up,

blowing the dust across the arid land in sinister spirals. The last flickering remnants of daylight were being extinguished and all contours disappeared in the greyish-brown, smothering gloom that was soon lashed by strong, unrelenting gusts. I crouched behind a rampart of tree stumps that had been bulldozed into long lines after the great hurricane. As darkness closed in from the horizon like a noose being tightened, I tried in vain to make out, through the swirling and ever denser obscurement, landmarks that a short while ago still stood out clearly, but with each passing moment the space around became more constricted. Even in my immediate vicinity I could soon not distinguish any line or shape at all. The mealy dust streamed from left to right, from right to left, to and fro on every side, rising on high and powdering down, nothing but a dancing grainy whirl for what must have been an hour, while further inland, as I later learnt, a heavy thunderstorm had broken. When the worst was over, the wavy drifts of sand that had buried the broken timber emerged from the gloom. Gasping for breath, my mouth and throat dry, I crawled out of the hollow that had formed around me like the last survivor of a caravan that had come to grief in the desert. A deathly silence prevailed. There was not a breath, not a birdsong to be heard, not a rustle, nothing. And although it now grew lighter once more, the sun, which was at its zenith, remained hidden behind the banners of pollen-fine dust that hung for a long time in the air. This, I thought, will be what is left after the earth has ground itself down. – I walked the rest of the way in a daze. All I remember is that my tongue was stuck to the roof of my mouth and that I felt as if I were walking on the spot. When at last I reached Orford, I climbed to the top of the castle keep, from where there is a view over the houses of the town, the green gardens and pallid fenlands, and the coastline to north and south, lost in the shimmering distance. Orford Castle was completed in 1165

and for centuries was the foremost bastion against the constant threat of invasion. Not until Napoleon was contemplating the conquest of the British Isles – his engineers audaciously planning to dig a tunnel under the Channel, and envisaging an armada of hot-air balloons advancing on the English coast – were new defensive measures taken, with the building of martello towers along the seashore, a mile or so apart. There are seven of these circular forts between Felixstowe and Orford alone. To the best of my knowledge, their effectiveness was never put to the test. The garrisons were soon withdrawn, and ever since these masonry shells have served as homes for the owls that make their soundless flights at dusk from the battlements. In the early Forties, the scientists and technicians at Bawdsey built radar masts along the east coast, eerie wooden structures more than eighty yards high which could sometimes be heard creaking in the night. No one knew what purpose they served any more than they knew about the many other secret projects then being pursued in the military research establishments around Orford. Naturally this gave rise to all manner of speculation about an invisible web of death rays, a new kind of nerve gas, or some hideous means of mass destruction that would come into play if the Germans attempted a landing. And it is a fact that until recently a file labelled *Evacuation of the Civil Population from Shingle Street, Suffolk* was in the archives of the Ministry of Defence, embargoed for seventy-five years as distinct from the usual practice of releasing documents after thirty, on the grounds that (so the irrepressible rumours claimed) it gave details of a horrifying incident in Shingle Street for which no government could accept public responsibility. I myself heard, for instance, that experiments were conducted at Shingle Street with biological weapons designed to make whole regions uninhabitable. I also heard tell of a system of pipes extending far out to sea, by means of which a petroleum inferno could be unleashed with such explosive rapidity, in the event of an invasion, that the very sea would start to boil. In the course of the preparatory experimentations, an entire company of English sappers were said to have met their deaths, inadvertently as it were, in the most appalling manner, according to eye witnesses who claimed to have seen the charred bodies, contorted with pain, lying on the beach or still out at sea in their boats. Others maintain that those who died in the wall of fire were German landing forces wearing English uniforms. When access to the Shingle Street file following a lengthy campaign was finally granted in 1992 in the local press, it revealed nothing that might have justified the top-secret classification, or

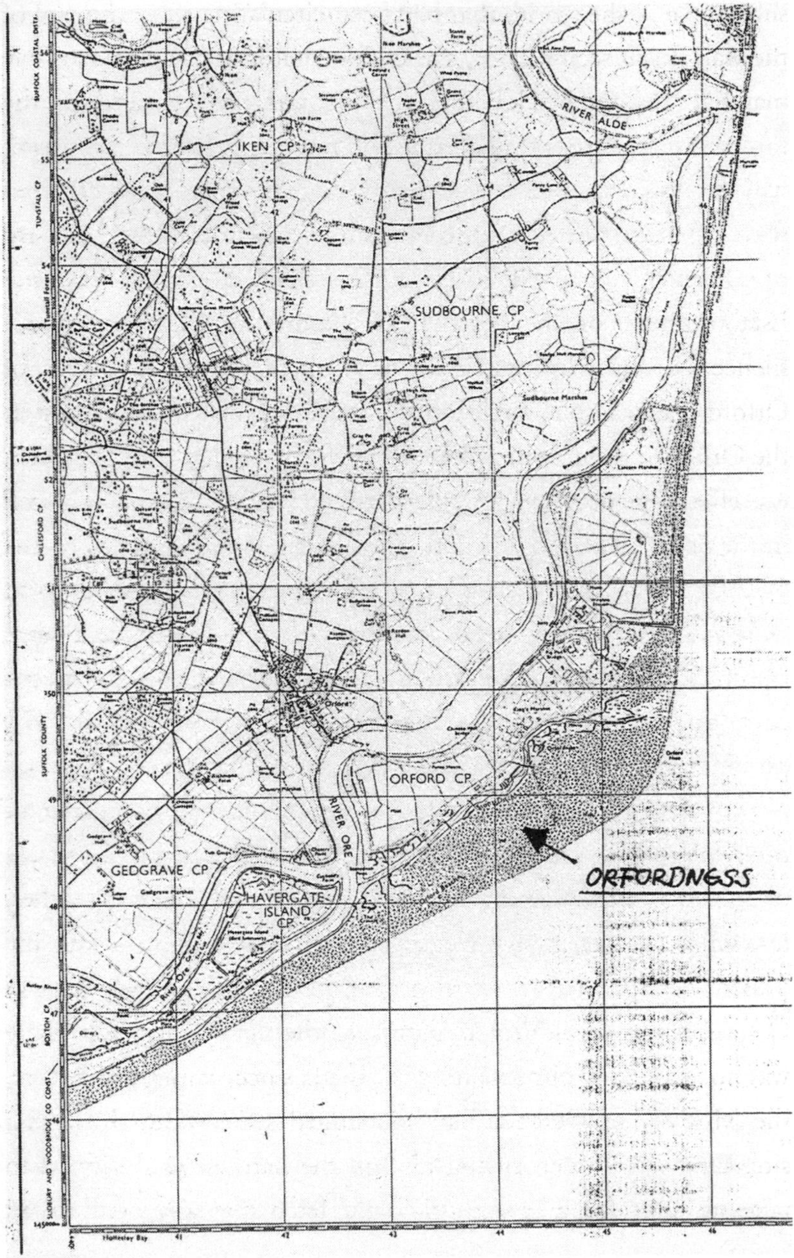

RIVER ALDE
IKEN CP
SUDBOURNE CP
Sudbourne Marshes
ORFORD CP
RIVER ORE
GEDGRAVE CP
HAVERGATE ISLAND CP
ORFORDNESS
SUFFOLK COASTAL DIST
TUNSTALL CP
CHILLESFORD CP
SUFFOLK COUNTY
BOYTON CP
SUDBURY AND WOODBRIDGE CO CONST
Hollesley Bay

substantiated the stories that had been circulating since the end of the war. But it seems likely, one commentator wrote, that sensitive material was removed before the file was opened, and so the mystery of Shingle Street remains. – Presumably part of the reason why rumours like this one concerning Shingle Street endured so obstinately was that, during the Cold War era, the Ministry of Defence continued to maintain Secret Weapons Research Establishments on the coast of Suffolk, and imposed the strictest silence on the work carried out in them. The inhabitants of Orford, for example, could only speculate about what went on at the Orfordness site, which, though perfectly visible from the town, was effectively no easier to reach than the Nevada desert or an atoll in the South Seas. For my part, I well recall standing down by the harbour when I first visited Orford in 1972 and looking across to what the locals simply called "the island", which resembled a penal colony in the Far East. I had been studying the curious coastal land formations at Orford on the map, and was interested in the promontory of Orfordness, which seemed to have an extra-territorial quality about it. Stone by stone, over a period of millennia, it had shifted down from the north across the mouth of the River Alde, in such a way that the tidal lower reaches, known as the Ore, run for some twelve miles just inside the present coastline before flowing into the sea. When I was first in Orford, it was forbidden to approach "the island", but now there was no longer any obstacle to going there, since, some years before, the Ministry of Defence had abandoned secret research at that site. One of the men sitting idly on the harbour wall offered to take me over for a few pounds and fetch me later after I had

had a look around. As we crossed the river in his blue-painted boat, he told me that people still mostly avoided Orfordness. Even the beach fishermen, who were no strangers to solitude, had given up night-fishing out there after a few attempts, allegedly because it wasn't worth their while, but in reality because they couldn't stand the god-forsaken loneliness of that outpost in the middle of nowhere, and in some cases even became emotionally disturbed for some time. Once we were on the other side, I took leave of my ferryman and, after climbing over the embankment, walked along a partially overgrown tarmac track running straight through a vast, yellowing field. The day was dull and oppressive, and there was so little breeze that not even the ears of the delicate quaking grass were nodding. It was as if I were passing through an undiscovered country, and I still remember that I felt, at the same time, both utterly liberated and deeply despondent. I had not a single thought in my head. With each step that I took, the emptiness within and the emptiness without grew ever greater and the silence more profound. Perhaps that was why I was frightened almost to death when a hare that had been hiding in the tufts of grass by the wayside started up, right at my feet, and shot off down the rough track before darting sideways, this way, then that, into the field. It must have been cowering there as I approached, heart pounding as it waited, until it was almost too late to get away with its life. In that very fraction of a second when its paralysed state turned into panic and flight, its fear cut right through me. I still see what occurred in that one tremulous instant with an undiminished clarity. I see the edge of the grey tarmac and every individual blade of grass, I see the hare leaping out of its hiding-place, with its ears laid back and a curiously human expression on its face that was rigid with terror and strangely divided; and in its eyes, turning to look back as it fled and almost popping out of its head with fright, I see myself, become one with it. Not till half-an-hour later, when I reached the broad dyke that separates the grass expanse from the pebble bank that slopes to the shoreline, did the blood cease its clamour in my veins. For a long while I stood on the bridge that leads to the former research establishment. Far behind me to the west,

scarcely to be discerned, were the gentle slopes of the inhabited land; to the north and south, in flashes of silver, gleamed the muddy bed of a dead arm of the river, through which now, at low tide, only a meagre trickle ran; and ahead lay nothing but destruction. From a distance, the concrete shells, shored up with stones,

in which for most of my lifetime hundreds of boffins had been at work devising new weapons systems, looked (probably because of their odd conical shape) like the tumuli in which the mighty and powerful were buried in prehistoric times with all their tools and utensils, silver and gold. My sense of being on ground intended for purposes transcending the profane was heightened by a number of buildings that resembled temples or pagodas,

which seemed quite out of place in these military installations. But the closer I came to these ruins, the more any notion of a mysterious isle of the dead receded, and the more I imagined myself amidst the remains of our own civilization after its extinction in some future catastrophe. To me too, as for some latter-day stranger ignorant of the nature of our society wandering about among heaps of scrap metal and defunct machinery, the beings who had once lived and worked here were an enigma, as was the purpose of the primitive contraptions and fittings inside the bunkers, the iron rails under the ceilings, the hooks on the still partially tiled walls, the showerheads the size of plates, the ramps and the soakaways. Where and in what time I truly was that day at Orfordness I cannot say, even now as I write these words. All I do know is that I finally walked along the raised embankment from the Chinese Wall Bridge past the old pumphouse towards the landing stage, to my left in the fading fields a collection of black Nissen huts, and to my right, across the river, the mainland. As I was sitting on the breakwater waiting for the ferryman, the evening sun emerged from behind the clouds, bathing in its light the far-reaching arc of the seashore. The tide was advancing up the river, the water was shining like tinplate, and from the radio masts high above the marshes came an even, scarcely audible hum. The roofs and towers of Orford showed among the tree tops, seeming so close that I could touch them. There, I thought, I was once at home. And then, through the growing dazzle of the light in my eyes, I suddenly saw, amidst the darkening colours, the sails of the long-vanished windmills turning heavily in the wind.

IX

After Orford, I headed inland travelling on one of the Eastern Counties Omnibus Company's red buses, going through Woodbridge to Yoxford where I set out on foot in a north-westerly direction along the old Roman road, into the thinly populated countryside that lies to the south of Harleston. I walked for nearly four hours, and in all that time I saw nothing apart from harvested cornfields stretching away into the distance under a sky heavy with clouds, and dark islands of trees surrounding the farmsteads which stood well back from the road, a mile or two apart from each other. I encountered hardly any vehicles while treading this seemingly unending straight, and I knew then as little as I know now whether walking in this solitary way was more of a pleasure or a pain. At times on that day, which I recall as being both leaden and unreal, a gap would open up among the billowing clouds. Then the rays of the sun would reach down to the earth, lighting up patches here and there and making a fan-shaped pattern as they descended, of the sort that used to appear in religious pictures symbolizing the presence above us of grace and providence. It was afternoon by the time

I came to the lane which leaves the Roman road across a cattle grid and leads through a meadow to Chestnut Tree Farm, an ancient moated house, where Thomas Abrams has been working on a model of the Temple of Jerusalem for a good twenty years. Now in his early sixties, Thomas Abrams has been a farmer all his life. He took to model-making soon after he left the village school, and like many of his kind he would spend the long winter evenings glueing little pieces of wood together to build all sorts of barques and sailing boats and famous ships such as the Cutty Sark and the Mary Rose. This pastime soon developed into a passion, and together with the interest he had long taken, as a Methodist lay preacher, in the factual basis of Biblical history, it gave him the idea, one evening towards the end of the Sixties, just as he was bedding the farm animals down for the night (so he told me), of recreating the Temple of Jerusalem exactly as it was at the beginning of our time. – Chestnut Tree Farm is a silent and somewhat sombrous place. Never yet, on my many visits, having come along the lane and crossed the little bridge over the moat to go up to the house, have I found anyone about. Even tapping with the heavy brass knocker brings nobody to the door. The big chestnut tree in the front yard, which must be several hundred years old, is motionless. Even the ducks on the water in the moat do not stir. If one takes a look inside through the window, it seems as if the mirror-bright dining table, the mahogany chest of drawers, the armchairs of burgundy red velvet, the hearth, and the ornaments and china figurines set out on the mantelpiece, had been drowsing there undisturbed for ever, so that one might well think that the owners have departed or died. But just as one is about to turn away, having waited and listened a while and feeling that one must have come at an inopportune moment, one sees Thomas Abrams waiting a little way off. And that is just how it was when I arrived there on foot from Yoxford on that late summer afternoon. As always, Thomas Abrams was wearing his green overalls and watchmaker's glasses. We exchanged a few words of no consequence as we walked to the barn in which the Temple was now nearing completion. Owing, however, to the size of the model, which covers nearly ten square yards, and to the minuteness and precision of the individual pieces, this process of completion is going so slowly that it is difficult to see any change from one year to the next, even though Thomas Abrams has almost given up farming, he told me, in order to be able to devote most of his time to the building of the Temple. He had just a few animals left, he said, and that more out of affection than any wish to profit from them. As I must have seen, the broad arable fields around the house had all been put back to pasture, and the standing hay was sold to one of his neighbours. It was ages since he had last driven a tractor. Hardly a day now passed that he did not work on the Temple for at least an hour or two. He had spent the past month painting about a hundred of the more than two thousand figures, no more than a quarter of an inch high, that peopled the Temple precincts. Then there are the alterations that need to be made, Thomas Abrams said, whenever my research leads to new findings. It is well known that archaeologists are divided amongst themselves as to the exact layout of the Temple; nor are my own often hard-gained insights always more reliable than the views of the squabbling scholars, even though my model is now thought to be the most accurate replica of the Temple ever produced. Thomas Abrams told me that he now received visitors from all over the world, historians from Oxford and Jehovah's Witnesses from Manchester, archaeological experts from the Holy Land, ultraorthodox Jews from London and representatives of evangelist sects from California, who had put to him the proposition that a full-size replica of the Temple should be built in the Nevada desert under his instructions. Various television companies and publishers were seeking to entice him, and Lord Rothschild had even offered to house the completed Temple in the entrance hall of his mansion near Aylesbury, and grant access to the public. The only advantage which had accrued to him personally as a result of the interest created by his work was that his neighbours, together with those members of his own family who had more or less openly expressed their doubts about whether he was of sound mind, were now a little more restrained in their disparaging comments. He could quite understand, said Thomas Abrams, how easy it was to consider someone barmy, who for so many years immersed himself deeper and deeper into a fantasy world and spent his time in an unheated barn fiddling about with such an apparently never ending, meaningless and pointless project, particularly when that same person was failing to look after his fields and to collect the subsidies he was entitled to. While the opinion of his neighbours, who had become fat on the senseless Brussels agricultural policy, had never concerned him much, the fact that it must at times have seemed to his wife and children that he was out of his mind was something that weighed on him rather more than he admitted. And so, he said, the day that Lord Rothschild drove into my yard in his limousine was indeed an important turning point in my life, because ever since then even the family have looked on me as a scholar engaged in serious study. On the other hand, of course, the constantly growing number of visitors keeps me from my work, and the work that still remains to be done is enormous. You might well say that because of my increasingly accurate knowledge, the task now seems in every respect more difficult to complete than ten or fifteen years ago. One of the American evangelists once asked me whether the Temple was inspired by divine revelation. And when I said to him it's nothing to do with divine revelation, he was very disappointed. If it had been divine revelation, I said to him, why would I have had to make alterations as I went along? No, it's just research really and work, endless hours of work, Thomas Abrams said. You had to study the Mishnah, he continued, and every other available source, and Roman architecture, and the distinctive features of the edifices raised by Herod in Masada and Borodium, because that was the only way of arriving at the right ideas. In the final analysis, our entire work is based on nothing but ideas, ideas which change over the years and which time and again cause one to tear down what one had thought to be finished, and begin again from scratch. I would more than likely never have started building the Temple if I had had any notion of how my work would get out of hand, and of the demands it would make on me as it became ever more complex. After all, if the Temple is to create the impression of being true to life, I have to make every one of the tiny coffers on the ceilings, every one of the hundreds of columns, and every single one of the many thousands of diminutive stone blocks by hand, and paint them as well. Now, as the edges of my field of vision are beginning to darken, I sometimes wonder if I will ever finish the Temple and whether all I have done so far has not been a wretched waste of time.

But on other days, when the evening light streams in through this window and I allow myself to be taken in by the overall view, then I see for a moment the Temple with its antechambers and the living quarters of the priesthood, the Roman garrison, the bath-houses, the market stalls, the sacrificial altars, covered walkways and the booths of the moneylenders, the great gateways and staircases, the forecourts and outer provinces and the mountains in the background, as if everything were already completed and as if I were gazing into eternity. In closing, Thomas Abrams dug out a magazine from under a pile of papers and showed me a double-page aerial view of the Temple precinct as it is today: white stones, dark cypresses, and in the centre, gleaming, the golden Dome of the Rock, which immediately brought to mind the dome of the new Sizewell reactor, which can be seen on moonlit nights shining like a shrine far across the land and sea. The Temple, Thomas Abrams said as we left his workshop, endured for only a hundred years. Perhaps this one will last a little longer. On the bridge over the moat, where we lingered for a while, Thomas Abrams told me how much he liked the ducks, a couple of which were quietly paddling around in the water and snapping up the food which he now and then took out of the pocket of his overalls and threw down for them. I have always kept ducks, he said, even as a child, and the colours of their plumage, in particular the dark green and snow white, seemed to me the only possible answer to the questions that are on my mind. That is how it has been for as long as I can remember. As I took my leave and mentioned that I had walked over from Yoxford and was now going on to Harleston, Thomas said that he would drive me as he had an errand in town anyway.

So we spent the quarter of an hour to Harleston sitting side by side in the cab of his truck, and I wished that the short drive through the country would never come to an end, that we could go on and on, all the way to Jerusalem. But instead I had to get out at the Saracen's Head in Harleston, an inn several centuries old whose guest rooms, as it transpired, were furnished with the most fearful pieces one can imagine. The headboard of the pink bed consisted of a black marbled formica construction nearly five feet high, with various drawers and compartments, rather like an altar; the thin-legged dressing-table was lavishly decorated with gold arabesques; and the mirror, which was fitted into the door of the wardrobe, made one look strangely deformed. As the wooden floorboards were very uneven and sloped towards the window, all the furniture stood at something of a tilt, so that I was pursued even while asleep by the feeling that the house was about to fall down. It was therefore with a certain relief that I left the Saracen's Head the following morning and walked eastward out of the town into the open fields. The stretch of land which I now traversed in a wide arc was no more densely populated than the one I journeyed through on the previous day. Every couple of miles there is a hamlet, and without exception these hamlets are named after the patron saints of their churches: St Mary and St Michael, St Peter, St James, St Andrew, St Lawrence, St John and St Cross, and as a result the people living there call the entire area The Saints. They say such things as: He bought land in The Saints, clouds are coming up over The Saints, that's somewhere out in The Saints and so on. My own feeling, as I walked over the featureless plain, was that I might well lose my bearings in The Saints, so often was I forced to change direction or strike out across country due to the labyrinthine system of footpaths and the many places where a right of way marked on the map had been ploughed up or was now overgrown. A couple of times I began to think I was lost, but then, around noon, I saw my goal, the round tower of the church of Ilketshall St Margaret, appear in the distance. Half an hour later I was sitting leaning against one of the gravestones in the cemetery of that parish, whose souls number no more today than in the Middle Ages. The eighteenth- and nineteenth-century parsons who were the incumbents of such remote livings usually dwelt with their families in the nearest small town and drove out into the country by pony cart just once or twice a week in order to hold services and make a few calls. One such vicar of Ilketshall St Margaret was the Reverend Ives, a mathematician and Hellenist of some standing, who lived with his wife and daughter in Bungay and was said to have liked his glass of sparkling Canary wine at dusk. During the summer of 1795 they were visited every day by a young French nobleman who had fled to England to escape the terrors of the Revolution. Ives talked with him about Homer's epics, Newton's mathematical theories, and the journeys which both of them had made in America. What great expanses that continent covered, and how immense the forests were, with trees whose trunks towered higher than the pillars of the tallest cathedrals! And the plunging waters of Niagara – what did their eternal thunder mean if there were not also someone standing at the edge of the cataract conscious of his forlornness in this world. Charlotte, the rector's fifteen-year-old daughter, would listen to these conversations with growing fascination, especially when their distinguished guest conjured up pictures in which warriors adorned with feathers appeared, and Indian maidens about whose dark skin there was a touch of moral pallor. Once she was so overcome with emotion that she ran out quickly into the garden on hearing of a hermit's good dog that led one such maiden, in her heart already a Christian, safely through the dangerous wilderness. When the teller of the tale later asked her what it was in his account that had so moved her, Charlotte answered that it was mainly the image of the dog carrying a lantern on a stick in his mouth, lighting the way through the night for the frightened Atala. It was always such little details rather than the lofty ideas that went straight to her heart. In the manner of such things, it was surely inevitable that the Vicomte, who was exiled from his homeland and undoubtedly surrounded by the aura of a romantic hero in Charlotte's eyes, took on the role of tutor and confidant as the weeks went by. Whilst it goes without saying that she practised her French, by taking dictation and engaging in conversation, Charlotte also asked her friend to devise more extensive courses of study for her, to include antiquity, the topography of the Holy Land, and Italian literature. They spent long hours in the afternoon together reading Tasso's *Gerusalemme Liberata* and the *Vita Nuova*, and in all likelihood there were times when the young girl's throat flushed scarlet and the Vicomte felt the thud of his heartbeat right under his jabot. Their day always ended with a music lesson. When dusk was settling inside the house, but the light streaming in from the west still lit the garden, Charlotte would play some piece or other from her repertoire, and the Vicomte, appuyé au bout du piano, would listen to her in silence. He was aware that their studies brought them closer every day, and, convinced that he was not fit to pick up her glove, sought to conduct himself with the utmost restraint, but nonetheless remained irresistibly drawn to her. With some dismay, as he later wrote in his *Mémoires d'outre-tombe*, I could foresee the moment at which I would be obliged to leave. The farewell dinner was a sad occasion during which no one knew what to say, and when it was over, much to the astonishment of the Vicomte, it was not the mother but the father who withdrew with Charlotte to the drawing room. Although he was on the point of departure, the mother – who, the Vicomte noticed, was herself most seductive in the unusual role which she was now playing in the teeth of convention – asked his hand in marriage for her daughter, whose heart, she said, was entirely his. You no longer have a native country, your property has been disposed of, your parents are no longer alive: what could possibly take you back to France? Stay here with us and be our adopted son and heir. The Vicomte, who could scarcely believe the generosity of this offer made to an impoverished emigrant, was thrown into the greatest conceivable inner turmoil by her proposal, which it seemed the Reverend Ives had approved. For while on the one hand, he wrote, he desired nothing so much as to be able to spend the rest of his life unknown to the world in the bosom of this solitary family, on the other hand the melodramatic moment had now come when he would have to disclose the fact that he was married. While the alliance he had entered into in France had been arranged by his sisters almost without consulting him and had remained a mere formality, this did not in the slightest alter the untenable situation in which he now found himself. Mme Ives had put her offer to him with her eyes half downcast, and when he responded with the despairing cry Arrêtez! Je suis marié! she fell into a swoon, and he was left with no other choice than to leave that hospitable house at once with the resolution never to return. Later, setting down his memories of that ill-omened day, he wondered how it would have been if he had undergone the transformation and led the life of a gentleman chasseur in that remote English county. It is probable that I should never have written a single word. In due course I should have even forgotten my own language. How great would France's loss have been, he asks, if I had vanished into thin air like that? And would it not, in the end, have been a better life? Is it not wrong to squander one's chance of happiness in order to indulge a talent? Will what I have written survive beyond the grave? Will there be anyone able to comprehend it in a world the very foundations of which are changed? – The Vicomte wrote these words in 1822. He was now the ambassador of the French king at the court of George IV. One morning, when he was sitting working in his study, his valet announced that a Lady Sutton had arrived in her carriage and wished to speak to him. When this strange caller crossed the threshold, accompanied by two boys aged about sixteen who, like herself, were in mourning, he had the impression that she found it difficult to remain upright owing to some inner agitation. The Vicomte took her by the hand and led her to an armchair. The two boys stood by her side. And the lady, speaking in a quiet, broken voice as she brushed back the black silk ribbons that hung from her bonnet, said: My lord, do you remember me? And I, the Vicomte wrote, recognised her. After twenty-seven years I was sitting at her side again, the tears swelled up in my eyes, and I saw her, through the veil of those tears, exactly as she had been during that summer which had long sunk into the shades of memory. Et vous, Madame, me reconnaissez-vous? I asked her. She did not reply, however, but looked at me with such a sad smile that I realized that we had meant far more to each other than I had admitted to myself at the time. – I am in mourning for my mother, she said; my father died years ago. As she said this, she withdrew her hand and covered her face. My children, she continued after some time, are the sons of Admiral Sutton, whom I married three years after you left us. You must excuse me now. I cannot say any more today. – She took my arm, the Vicomte writes in his memoirs, and as I led her through the house, down the stairs and back to her carriage, I held her hand against my heart and could feel that she was trembling. She drove off with her two dark-haired boys sitting opposite her like two mute servants. Quel bouleversement des destinées! Over the next few days, the Vicomte writes, I visited Lady Sutton four times at the address in Kensington that she had given me. On none of these occasions were her sons at home. We talked and were silent, and with each Do you remember? our past life rose more clearly from the cruel abyss of time. On my fourth visit, Charlotte asked me to put in a good word with George Canning, who had just been made Governor-General of India, for the elder of her two sons, who planned to go to Bombay. It was solely on account of this request, she said, that she had come to London, and she must now return to Bungay. Farewell! I shall never see you again! Farewell! – After this painful parting I spent long hours shut away in my study at the embassy and, with repeated interruptions for vain reflection and brooding, committed our unhappy story to paper. As I did so, I was troubled by the question of whether in the writing I should not once again betray and lose Charlotte Ives, and this time for ever. But the fact is that writing is the only way in which I am able to cope with the memories which overwhelm me so frequently and so unexpectedly. If they remained locked away, they would become heavier and heavier as time went on, so that in the end I would succumb under their mounting weight. Memories lie slumbering within us for months and years, quietly proliferating, until they are woken by some trifle and in some strange way blind us to life. How often this has caused me to feel that my memories, and the labours expended in writing them down are all part of the same humiliating and, at bottom, contemptible business! And yet, what would we be without memory? We would not be capable of ordering even the simplest thoughts, the most sensitive heart would lose the ability to show affection, our existence would be a mere never-ending chain of meaningless moments, and there would not be the faintest trace of a past. How wretched this life of ours is! – so full of false conceits, so futile, that it is little more than the shadow of the chimeras loosed by memory. My sense of estrangement is becoming more and more dreadful. When I walked in Hyde Park yesterday, I felt unspeakably wretched and outcast amongst the colourful crowd. As if from afar, I watched the beautiful young English women with the same ardent bewilderment of my senses that I used to feel in an embrace. And today I do not raise my eyes from my work. I have become almost invisible, to some extent like a dead man. Perhaps that is why it appears to me that this world which I have very nearly left behind is shrouded in some peculiar mystery.

The story of Charlotte Ives is only a minute fragment of the several thousand pages of the Vicomte de Chateaubriand's memoirs. It was in Rome in 1806 that he first felt the desire to search the depths of his soul. In 1811, Chateaubriand began this undertaking in earnest, and from that time onwards he devoted himself to his recollections whenever the circumstances of his at once glorious and painful life permitted. His personal feelings and thoughts unfolded against the background of the momentous upheavals of those years: the Revolution, the Reign of Terror, his own exile, the rise and fall of Napoleon, the Restoration and the July Monarchy all were part of this interminable play performed upon the world's stage, a play which took its toll on the privileged observer no less than on the nameless masses. The scene was constantly changing. We see the coast of Virginia from on board a ship, visit the naval arsenal in Greenwich, marvel at his description of the great fire of Moscow, stroll through the parks of Bohemian spas and witness the bombardment of Thionville. Burning torches illuminate the city battlements, which are swarming with thousands of soldiers; the fiery trajectories of cannonballs criss-cross the dark air; and before each report from the guns, a dazzling glare lights up the towering clouds in the sky right up to the blue zenith. At times the noise of the battle dies down for a few seconds, and then one can hear the beating of drums, brass fanfares, and orders bellowed out by voices strained to breaking point. *Sentinelles, prenez garde à vous!* Within the overall context of the task of remembering, such colourful accounts of military spectacles and large-scale operations form what might be called the highlights of history which staggers blindly from one disaster to the next.

The chronicler, who was present at these events and is once more recalling what he witnessed, inscribes his experiences, in an act of self-mutilation, onto his own body. In the writing, he becomes the martyred paradigm of the fate Providence has in store for us, and, though still alive, is already in the tomb that his memoirs represent. From the very outset, recapitulating the past can have only one end, the hour of deliverance, which in the case of Chateaubriand came on the 4th of June 1848, the day on which death took the pen from his hand in a rez-de-chaussée in the Rue du Bac. Combourg, Rennes, Brest, St Malo, Philadelphia, New York, Boston, Brussels, the island of Jersey, London, Beccles and Bungay, Milan, Verona, Venice, Rome, Naples, Vienna, Berlin, Potsdam, Constantinople, Jerusalem, Neuchâtel, Lausanne, Basle, Ulm, Waldmünchen, Teplitz, Karlsbad, Prague and Pilsen, Bamberg, Würzburg and Kaiserslautern, and time and again, Versailles, Chantilly, Fontainebleau, Rambouillet, Vichy and Paris – these were just a few of the stations along a journey which had now reached its end. At the beginning was a childhood in Combourg, the account of which became indelibly imprinted on my mind the very first time I read it. François-René was the youngest of ten children, the first four of whom lived for no more than a few months. The others were christened Jean-Baptiste, Marie-Anne, Bénigne, Julie and Lucile. All four girls were of a rare beauty, especially Julie and Lucile, both of whom were to die in the turmoil of the Revolution. The Chateaubriand family lived in total seclusion, with a number of servants, in the manor house at Combourg, where the halls and passages were so vast and endless that an army of crusaders might lose their way in them. Apart from a few neighbouring noblemen such as the Marquis de Monlouet or Count Goyon-Beaufort, no one ever visited the castle. Particularly in winter, Chateaubriand writes, entire months would pass without any travellers or strangers knocking on the gate of our fortress. Far greater than the sadness that hung over the surrounding heath was the sadness that pervaded this lonely house. Those who walked beneath its vaults felt much as one might when entering a Carthusian monastery. The bell for dinner always rang at eight. After dinner, we would sit for a few hours by the fire. The wind would be moaning in the chimney, mother sighed on the sofa, and father, whom I never saw seated except at table, paced up and down the enormous dining hall until it was time for bed. He always wore a white woollen shaggy robe, and a cap of the same material. Once he was at a certain distance from the centre of the hall, which was lit only by the flickering fire in the hearth and a solitary candle, he would begin to disappear into the shadows, and, when he was completely immersed in the darkness, all one would hear was his footfall until he came back like a ghost, in his peculiar attire. During the summer months, we would sit outside on the steps in front of the house as it was getting dark. Father would fire his shotgun at owls, and we children and mother would look across at the black tree tops of the forest and up at the heavens where the stars came out one by one. At the age of seventeen, Chateaubriand writes, I left Combourg. One day my father pronounced that I would have to make my own way henceforth. He had determined that I would join the Régiment de Navarre and leave on the following day to travel to Cambrai via Rennes. Here, he said, are a hundred Louis d'or. Do not squander them and never dishonour your name. At the time of my departure he was already suffering from the progressive paralysis which was finally to send him to his grave. His left arm twitched constantly, and he had to keep it still with his right hand. And that was how, after he had given me his old rapier, he stood with me beside the cabriolet that was already waiting in the green courtyard. We drove up the lane by the fishponds, and one more time I beheld the mill stream shining and the swallows swooping across the reeds. Then I looked ahead, at the broad terrain that was now opening up in front of me.

It took another hour to walk from Ilketshall St Margaret to Bungay, and a further hour from Bungay over the marshes of the Waveney valley to the far side of Ditchingham. Visible from a distance, nestling at the foot of the ridge which drops down quite steeply to the watermeadows, was Ditchingham Lodge, the isolated house where Charlotte Ives lived for many years after her marriage to Admiral Sutton. As I approached, I could see the window panes glinting in the sunlight. A woman in a white apron – what an unusual sight, I thought – came out underneath the portico roof which was supported by two columns, calling a black dog that was running about in the garden. Apart from her there was not a soul in sight. I climbed the slope to the main road and then walked across the stubble fields to Ditchingham churchyard, some way outside the village, where the elder of Charlotte's two sons, who went to seek his fortune in Bombay, is buried. The inscription on the stone sarcophagus reads: At Rest Beneath, 3rd Feb^{ry} 1850, Samuel Ives Sutton, Eldest Son of Rear Admiral Sutton, Late Captain 1st Battalion 60th Rifles, Major by Brevét and Staff Officer of Pentioners. Next to Samuel Sutton's grave stands another even more imposing monument, also built of slabs of heavy stone and crowned by an urn. What struck me about this tomb were the round holes on the upper edges of the four sides. They reminded me somehow of the air-holes we used to make as children in the lids of the boxes in which we kept the cockchafers we caught, with some leaves for food. It was possible, I thought to myself, that the bereaved had had these holes bored into the stone in the eventuality that the dear departed in her sepulchre should wish once more

to breathe the air. The name of the lady who had been cared for in this manner was Sarah Camell, who died on the 26th of October 1799. As the wife of the Ditchingham doctor, she would have been acquainted with the Ives family, and it is probable that Charlotte, together with her parents, was present at the funeral and perhaps even played a pavane on the pianoforte at the Camells' home after the service. The higher sentiments which were cultivated at the time in the circles in which Sarah and Charlotte moved are preserved in the elegant words of the epitaph which Dr Camell, who survived his wife by nearly forty years, had engraved on the south-facing side of the pale grey tomb:

Firm in the principles and constant
in the practice of religion
Her life displayed the peace of virtue
Her modest sense, Her unobtrusive elegance
of mind and manners,
Her sincerity and benevolence of heart
Secured esteem, conciliated affection,
Inspired confidence and diffused happiness.

Ditchingham churchyard was very the last stop on my walk through the county of Suffolk. The afternoon was already drawing to a close, and so I decided to return to the main road and continue a short way in the direction of Norwich, to the Mermaid in Hedenham, where the bar would be opening soon. I would be able to phone home from there to be picked up. The route I had to take led me past Ditchingham Hall, a house built around 1700 in beautiful mauve-coloured brick, the windows of which are fitted with dark green shutters. It was situated well off the main road above a serpentine lake, and encompassed on all sides by extensive parkland. Later, while I was waiting for Clara in the Mermaid, it occurred to me that Ditchingham Park must have been laid out around the time when Chateaubriand was in Suffolk. Estates of this kind, which enabled the ruling elite to imagine themselves surrounded by boundless lands where nothing offended the eye, did not become fashionable until the second half of the eighteenth century. Planning and executing the work necessary for an emparkment could take two or three decades. In order to complete such a project it was usually necessary to buy parcels of land and add them to the existing estate, and roads, tracks, individual farmsteads, sometimes even entire villages had to be moved, as the object was to enjoy an uninterrupted view from the house over a natural expanse innocent of any human presence. It was for the same reason that fences were replaced with broad, grass-covered ha-has, which were dug out at a cost of many thousands of working hours. Naturally, such an undertaking, with its considerable impact not only on the landscape, but also on the life of the local communities, could not always be accomplished without controversy. At the period in question, an ancestor of Earl Ferrers, the present owner of Ditchingham Hall, having become embroiled in a confrontation with one of his estate managers, dispatched him with his gun, for which deed he was in due course sentenced to death by his peers in the House of Lords, and hanged publicly in London by a silken rope. – The least costly aspect of laying out a landscaped park was planting trees as specimens or in small groups, even if it was not seldom preceded by the felling of tracts of woodland and the burning-off of unsightly thickets and scrub that did not comply with the overall concept. Nowadays, given that only a third of the trees planted at the time are still standing in most parks, and that more are dying each year of old age and many other causes, we will soon be able to envisage once more the Torricelli-like emptiness in which the great country seats stood in the late eighteenth century. Chateaubriand also later made a modest attempt to realize the ideal of nature projected into that emptiness. When he returned in 1807 from his long journey to Constantinople and Jerusalem, he bought a summer house that lay hidden among wooded hills in the Vallée aux Loups, not far from the town of Aulnay. It is there that he begins to write his memoirs, on the first pages of which he speaks of the trees he has planted and tended with his own hands. Now, he says, they are still so small that I provide them with shade whenever I step between them and the sun. But one day, when they have grown, they will give shade to me, and look after me in my old age much as I looked after them in their youth. I feel a bond unites me with these trees; I write sonnets, elegies and odes to them; they are like children, I know them all by name, and my only desire is that I should end my days amongst them. – This picture was taken at

Ditchingham about ten years ago, on a Saturday afternoon when the manor house was open to the public in aid of charity. The Lebanese cedar which I am leaning against, unaware still of the woeful events that were to come, is one of the trees that were planted when the park was laid out, and most of which, as I have said, have already disappeared. Since the mid-Seventies there has been an ever more rapid decline in the numbers of trees, with heavy losses, above all amongst the species most common in England. Indeed, one tree has become well nigh extinct: Dutch elm disease spread from the south coast into Norfolk around 1975, and within the space of just two or three summers there were no elms left alive in the vicinity. The six elm trees which had shaded the pond in our garden withered away in June 1978, just a few weeks after they unfolded their marvellous light green foliage for the last time. The virus spread through the root systems of entire avenues with unbelievable speed, causing capillaries to tighten and leading to the trees' dying of thirst. Even solitary trees were located with infallible accuracy by the airborne beetles which spread the disease. One of the most perfect trees I have ever seen was an almost two hundred-year-old elm that stood on its own in a field not far from our house. About one hundred feet tall, it filled an immense space. I recall that, after most of the elms in the area had succumbed, its countless, somewhat asymmetrical, finely serrated leaves would sway in the breeze as if the scourge which had obliterated its entire kind would pass it by without a trace; and I also recall that a bare fortnight later all these apparently invincible leaves were brown and curled up, and dust before the autumn came. It was then also that I noticed that the crowns of ash trees were becoming sparse, and the foliage of oaks was thinning and displaying strange mutations. At the same time, the trees themselves were producing leaves from hard old wood, and by mid-summer they were dropping masses of rock-hard, deformed acorns that were covered with a sticky substance. The beech trees, which until then had remained in good shape, were affected by several long droughts. The leaves were only half their usual size, and almost all the beechnuts were empty. One after the other, the poplars on the meadow died. Some of the dead

trunks are still standing, while others lie broken and bleached in the grass. Finally, in the autumn of 1987, a hurricane such as no one had ever experienced before passed over the land. According to official estimates over fourteen million mature hard-leaf trees fell victim to it, not to mention the damage to conifer plantations and bushes. That was on the night of the 16th of October. Without warning, the storm came up out of the Bay of Biscay, moved along the French west coast, crossed the English Channel and swept over the south-east part of the island out into the North Sea. I woke at about three in the morning, less as a result of the thunderous roar than because of the curious warmth and the increasing air pressure in my bedroom. In contrast with other equinoctial gales which I have experienced here, this one came not in driving gusts but with an unrelenting and, it seemed, ever more powerful force. I stood at the window and looked through the glass, which was strained almost to breaking point, down towards the end of the garden, where the crowns of the large trees in the neighbouring bishop's park were bent and streaming like aquatic plants in a deep current. White clouds raced across in the darkness, and again and again the sky was lit up by a terrible flickering which, I later discovered, was caused by power lines touching each other. At some point I must have turned away for a while. At all events, I still remember that I did not believe my eyes when I looked out again and saw that where the currents of air had shortly beforehand been pouring through the black mass of trees, there was now just the paleness of the empty horizon. It seemed as if someone had pulled a curtain to one side to reveal a formless scene that bordered upon the underworld. And at the very moment that I registered the unaccustomed brightness of the night over the park, I knew that everything down there had been destroyed. And yet I hoped that the ghastly emptiness could be explained by some other means, for in the mounting din of the storm I had heard none of the crashing sounds that go with the felling of timber. It was not until later that I realized that the trees, held to the last by their root systems, toppled only gradually, and because they were forced down so slowly their crowns, which were entangled with each other, did not shatter but remained virtually undamaged. In this way, entire tracts of woodland were pressed down flat as if they had been cornfields. In the first light of dawn, when the storm had begun to abate, I ventured out into the garden. For a long time I stood choked with emotion amidst the devastation. It was like being in a kind of wind tunnel, so strong was the suction created by the onrushing air, which was far too warm for the time of year. The ancient trees on either side of the path leading along the edge of the park were all lying on the ground as if in a swoon, and beneath the huge oaks, ash and plane trees, beeches and limes lay the torn and mangled shrubs that had grown in their shade, thujas and yews, hazel and laurel bushes, holly and rhododendrons. With pulsating radiance the sun rose over the horizon. The gusts continued for a while, and then it was suddenly quiet. Nothing moved, apart from the birds which had lived in the bushes and trees and which were now flitting about amongst the branches that had remained green well into the autumn that year. I do not know how I got through the first day after the storm, but do recall that during the night, doubting what I had seen with my own eyes, I walked once more through the park. As there were power cuts throughout the whole region, everything was in deep darkness. There was no glare from street-lights or houses to dull the sky. But the stars had come out, in a display so resplendent as I had seen only over the Alps when I was a child, or over the desert in my dreams. From the extreme north right down to the south where the view had before been blocked by trees, the sparkling constellations were spread out, the Plough, the tail of Draco, the triangle of Taurus, the Pleiades, Pegasus, the Swan and the Dolphin. Unchanged and, it seemed to me, more magnificent than ever before, they revolved above me.

The silence of that brilliant night after the storm was followed by the revving of chainsaws during the winter months. It took four or five labourers until March to cut up the branches, burn the rubbish, and haul away the trunks. An excavator dug large holes in which stumps and roots, some of them the size of a small house, were buried. Now, in the truest sense of the word, everything was turned upside down. The forest floor, which in the spring of last year had still been carpeted with snowdrops, violets and wood anemones, ferns and cushions of moss, was now covered by a layer of barren clay. All that grew in the hard-baked earth were tufts of swamp grass, the seeds of which had lain in the depths for goodness knew how long. The rays of the sun, with nothing left to impede them, destroyed all the shade-loving plants so that it seemed as if we were living on the edge of an infertile plain. Where a short while ago the dawn chorus had at times reached such a pitch that we had to close the bedroom windows, where larks had risen on the morning air above the fields and where, in the evenings, we occasionally even heard a nightingale in the thicket, its pure and penetrating song punctuated by theatrical silences, there was now not a living sound.

X

Amongst the miscellaneous papers left by Sir Thomas Browne treating such diverse subjects as practical and ornamental horticulture, the urns found at Brampton in Norfolk, the making of artificial hills and burrows, the several plants mentioned in Scripture, the Saxon tongue, the pronouncements of the Oracle at Delphos, the fishes eaten by our Saviour, the behaviour of insects, hawks and falconry, and a case of boulimia centenaria which occurred in Yarmouth, amongst these and various other tracts, there is also to be found a catalogue of remarkable books,

MUSÆUM CLAUSUM

or

Bibliotheca Abscondita

listing pictures, antiquities and sundry singular items that may have formed part of a collection put together by Browne but were more likely products of his imagination, the inventory of a treasure-house that existed purely in his head and to which there is no access except through the letters on the page. In a short prefatory note to an unknown reader, Browne compares this "Musæum Clausum" with the Musæum Aldrovandi, the Musæum Calceolarianum; the Casa Abbellita at Loretto, and the repositories of the Emperor Rudolf at Prague and Vienna, all of them famed collections of his day. Among the rare books and documents in Browne's "Musæum" are King Solomon's treatise on the shadow cast by our thoughts, *de Umbris Idœarum*, previously reported to have been in the library of the Duke of Bavaria; a collection of Hebrew epistles, which passed between the two most learned women of the seventeenth century, Molinea of Sedan and Maria Schurman of Utrecht; and "a Sub Marine Herbal" describing in exhaustive detail all that grows on the mountain ranges and in the valleys under the sea, the many kinds of algae, corals and waterferns never seen by man, sargassum borne along by tropical currents, as well as whole islands of plants drifting from continent to continent in the path of the trade winds. Browne's imaginary library further includes a fragment of an account by the ancient traveller Pytheas of Marseilles, referred to in Strabo, according to which all the air beyond Thule is thick, condensed and gellied, looking just like sea lungs, and moreover a poem by Ovidius Naso, hitherto supposed lost, written in the Getick language during his exile at Tomi and found wrapt up in wax at Sabaria, on the frontiers of Hungary, where there remains a tradition that he died in his return towards Rome from Tomi, either after his pardon or the death of Augustus. Apart from all manner of other curiosities, Browne's museum has in it a drawing in chalk of the great fair of Almachara in Arabia, which is held at night to avoid the great heat of the sun; a painting of the famous battle fought between the Romans and the Jaziges on the frozen Danube; a dream image showing a prairie or sea meadow at the bottom of the Mediterranean, off the coast of Provence; Solyman the Magnificent on horseback at the siege of Vienna, and behind him a whole city of snow-white tents extending as far as the horizon; a seascape with floating icebergs upon which sit walruses, bears, foxes and a variety of rare fowls; and a number of pieces delineating the worst inhumanities in tortures for the benefit of the observer: the scaphismus of the Persians, the living truncation of the Turks, the hanging sport at the feasts of the Thracians, the exact method of flaying men alive, beginning between the shoulders, according to the meticulous description of Thomas Minadoi. Occupying some undefined position between the natural and the unnatural is also a fair English lady drawn al negro, or in the Æthiopian hue excelling the original white beauty, with the motto: "Sed quandam volo nocte nigriorem". In addition to such astonishing writings and artworks, the Musæum Clausum also contains medals and coins; a precious stone from a vulture's head; a neat crucifix made out of the crossbone of a frog's head; ostrich and humming-bird eggs; bright-hued parakeet feathers; spirits and salt of Sargasso excellent against the scurvy; extract of cachundè or liberans employed in the East Indies against melancholy; and a glass of spirits made of æthereal salt, hermetically sealed up, of so volatile a nature that it will not endure daylight, and therefore shown only in winter, or by the light of a carbuncle, or Bononian stone. All of these things are recorded by Browne the doctor and naturalist in his register of marvels, all of these and many more that I do not propose to list in this place, excepting perhaps the bamboo cane in which, at the time of the Byzantine Emperor Justinianus, two Persian friars who had long been in China to discover the secrets of sericulture had brought the first eggs of the silkworm over the Empire's borders into the Western world.

The silkworm moth, *Bombyx mori*, which lives in white-fruited mulberry trees is a member of the *Bombycidae* or spinners, a subspecies of the *Lepidoptera* which, together with the *Saturnidae*, includes some of the most beautiful of all moths – the Kentish Glory, *Endromis versilcolor*, the Great Peacock, *Bombyx atlas*, the Large Ermine, *Harpyia vinula* and the Emperor moth, *Saturnia pavonia.* The fully developed silkworm moth, however, is an unprepossessing creature measuring a mere one and a half

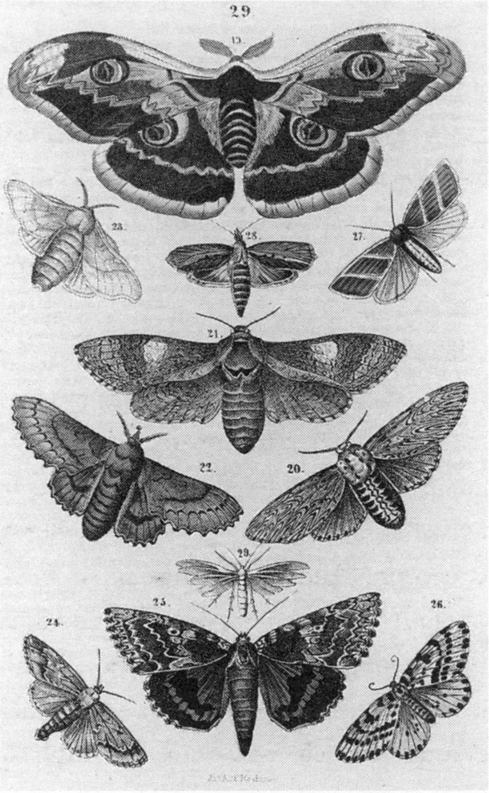

inches across and an inch lengthways. Its wings are ashen white with pale brown stripes and a crescent-shaped, often barely perceptible mark. The only purpose it has is to propagate. The male dies soon after mating. The female lays three to five hundred eggs over the course of several days, and then also dies. The silkworms that hatch from the eggs, an encyclopaedia dating from 1844 informs me, are enrobed in a black, velvety fur when they enter this world. During their short lives, which last only six or seven weeks, they are overcome by sleep on four occasions and, after shedding their old skin, emerge from each one re-made, always whiter, smoother and larger, becoming more beautiful, and finally almost completely transparent. A few days after the last sloughing one can notice a redness on the throat, which heralds the onset of metamorphosis. The caterpillar now stops eating, runs about restlessly, and, seeking to leave the low earth behind, strives to gain greater heights, until it has found the right place and can start to weave its cell from the resinous juices produced in its insides. If one slits open a caterpillar that has been killed with ethyl alcohol along the length of its back, one sees a cluster of intertwined small tubes that resemble intestines. They end by the mouth, in two very fine orifices, through which the juices pour forth. During its first day of work, the caterpillar spins an extensive, disorderly, fragmented web which is used to secure the cocoon. And then, constantly moving its head back and forth and reeling out an uninterrupted thread almost a thousand yards long, it constructs the actual egg-shaped casing around itself. In this shell, which admits neither air nor moisture, the caterpillar changes into a nymph by sloughing off its skin for one last time. It remains in this state for two to three weeks in all, until the butterfly described above emerges. – The silkworm's native habitat seems to include all those Asian countries where the white mulberry trees grow in the wild. There it lived in the open, left to its own devices, until man, having discovered its usefulness, was prompted to foster it. Chinese history notes that, two thousand and seven hundred years before the beginning of the Christian calendar, Huang Ti, the Emperor of the Earth who reigned for more than a century and taught his subjects how to build wagons, ships and grain mills, persuaded his first wife, Hsi-ling-shi, to attend to the silkworms, to devise trials for their employment, and increase, by means of this her especial task, the happiness of the people. Hsi-ling-shi thereupon took the worms from the trees in the palace garden and into her own care, in the imperial apartments, where, protected from their natural enemies and the unpredictable and often inclement spring weather, they thrived so well that this marked the beginning of what was later to be developed into domestic silkworm culture. Together with the unravelling of the cocoons and the weaving and embroidering of the materials, this was to become the principal occupation of all the succeeding empresses, and passed from their hands into those of the entire female sex. Promoted in every conceivable way by those in authority, the rearing of silkworms and the production of silk had, in the course of a few generations, taken such an upturn that the name of China came to be synonymous with an inexhaustible wealth of silk. Chinese merchants traversed the length and breadth of Asia with their silk-laden caravans, taking some two hundred and forty days to travel from the Chinese sea to the coast of the Mediterranean. Because of this enormous distance, and also because of the horrific punishments awaiting those who disseminated the knowledge of sericulture beyond the borders of the Empire, the fabrication of silk was restricted to China for thousands of years, until the two aforementioned friars with their hollowed-out walking staffs arrived in Byzantium. After the raising of silkworms had become established at the Greek court and on the Aegean islands, it took a further millennium for this elaborate form of husbandry to pass via Sicily and Naples to Piedmont, Savoy and Lombardy, where Genoa and Milan soon flourished as the European centres of silk cultivation. Within half a century, the art of silk-making had reached France from northern Italy, thanks to Olivier de Serres, who is still considered the father of French agriculture. His manual for landowners, published in 1600 under the title *Théatre d'agriculture et mesnage de Champs*, which went through thirteen printings in a very short space of time, made such a deep impression on Henry IV that he summoned him to Paris, offering him copious honours and favours, to be his first counsellor, on a par with Sully, his prime minister and minister of finance. De Serres, who was reluctant to surrender the management of his own estates to someone else, demanded one favour as a condition for accepting the office he had been offered: that the cultivation of silk should be introduced in France, and that to that end the native trees in the royal gardens throughout the country be uprooted and mulberry trees planted in their stead. The king was enthralled by de Serres' plan, but before it could be put into practice he had to overcome the resistance of Sully, whom he normally held in high esteem and who opposed the idea of producing silk, either because he genuinely considered it the height of folly or because he saw in de Serres a rival in the ascendant.

The arguments which Maximilien de Béthune, Duc de Sully, brought to bear with his sovereign are summed up in the sixteenth volume of his memoirs, a fine edition of which, printed in 1788 by

MÉMOIRES
DE SULLY.

LIVRE SEIZIÈME.

IL ne s'agiſſoit plus que de donner une dernière forme aux conventions qui ve- 1603.

F. J. Desoer in Liège, à la Croix d'or, I acquired for a few shillings many years ago at an auction in the small country town of Aylsham, north of Norwich. Sully opened his case by maintaining that the French climate was unsuited to producing silk. The spring, so Sully asserted, began too late, and even when it did arrive, humidity, rising out of the fields or descending on them, tended to be too high. This unfavourable circumstance alone, which nothing could countervail, was extremely detrimental both to the silkworms, which could only with great difficulty be persuaded to hatch, and to the mulberry trees, which needed mild air above all else, especially at that time of year when they were coming into leaf, if they were to flourish. Quite apart from this basic consideration, Sully continued, one had to bear in mind that rural life in France allowed nobody any superfluous leisure, with the possible exception of the habitually idle; and therefore, if one really were to introduce silk cultivation on a large scale, one would have to prevent rural labourers from going about their accustomed daily work and employ them in what was in every respect a dubious enterprise. Sully conceded that country folk would in all likelihood be easily persuaded to make such a change in their basic way of life, for who would not give up labouring on the land for a venture like silk cultivation, which required no real effort at all? And therein lay the most compelling reason against a general adoption of sericulture in France, urged Sully in a deft turn of phrase directed at the soldier king: the danger that the rural population, from whom the best musketeers and cavalrymen had always been recruited, would lose their innate vigour by being employed on work more fitting for women's and children's hands. As a result, it would soon no longer be possible to ensure that among the next generations there would be sufficient numbers of men capable of practising the martial arts. And not only would the manufacturing of silk lead to degeneration among the country folk, Sully continued, but it would also promote the insidious corruption of the urban classes through luxurious living and all that went with it – laziness, effeminacy, lechery and extravagance. Far too much was already being lavished in France on ornamental gardens and ostentatious palaces, on the most extravagant furnishings and décor, gold ornaments and porcelain, carriages and cabriolets, galas and festivities, liqueurs and perfumes, and even, Sully noted, on public offices sold at exorbitant prices, and marriageable ladies from the upper classes, who were auctioned off to the highest bidder. Further to encourage the general decline in moral standards by introducing silk cultivation throughout the kingdom was something Sully must advise his King against, and, par contre, he wished to suggest that one might now like to remember the virtues of those who sustained themselves in the most modest and frugal way. However, the prime minister's objections were ignored, and silk cultivation became established in France within a decade, not least because the Edict of Nantes, which was proclaimed in 1598, safeguarded at least a degree of tolerance to the Huguenots, who until that time had been subject to severe persecution, thereby making it possible for the very people who had played a prominent part in introducing silk cultivation to remain in their French fatherland. – Inspired by the French example, the adoption of silk cultivation by royal patronage occurred at almost the same time in England. On the site where Buckingham Palace now stands, James I had a mulberry garden of several acres laid out, and at Theobald's, his favourite country seat in Essex, he maintained his own silk house for the rearing of silkworms. James was so greatly interested in these industrious creatures that he would spend hour after hour studying their habits and needs, and whenever he undertook journeys about his kingdom he always had with him a large casket full of royal silkworms, the keeping of which was entrusted to a specially appointed groom of the chamber. James had well over a hundred thousand mulberry trees planted in the drier counties of eastern England, and in this and other ways he laid the foundations for an important branch of industry which entered its heyday at the beginning of the eighteenth century, when, following the revocation of the Edict of Nantes by Louis XIV, more than fifty thousand Huguenots fled to England, many of whom, experienced in breeding silkworms and in the fabrication of silk stuffs – craftsmen and merchant families such as the Lefèvres and the Tillettes, the De Hagues, the Martineaus and the Columbines – settled in Norwich, at that time the second largest city in England, where since the early sixteenth century there had been a colony of about five thousand immigrant Flemish and Walloon weavers. By 1750, a bare two generations later, the Huguenot master weavers of Norwich had risen to become the wealthiest, most influential and cultivated class of entrepreneurs in the entire kingdom. In their factories and those of their suppliers there was the greatest imaginable commotion, day in, day out, and it is said in a history of silk manufacture in England that a traveller approaching Norwich under the black sky of a winter night would be amazed by the glare over the city, caused by light coming from the windows of the workshops, still busy at this late hour. Increase of light and increase of labour have always gone hand in hand. If today, when our gaze is no longer able to penetrate the pale reflected glow over the city and its environs, we think back to the eighteenth century, it hardly seems possible that even then, before the Industrial Age, a great number of people, at least in some places, spent their lives with their wretched bodies strapped to looms made of wooden frames and rails, hung with weights, and reminiscent of instruments of torture or cages. It was a

peculiar symbiosis which, perhaps because of its relatively primitive character, makes more apparent than any later form of factory work that we are able to maintain ourselves on this earth only by being harnessed to the machines we have invented. That weavers in particular, together with scholars and writers with whom they had much in common, tended to suffer from melancholy and all the evils associated with it, is understandable given the nature of their work, which forced them to sit bent over, day after day, straining to keep their eye on the complex patterns they created. It is difficult to imagine the depths of despair into which those can be driven who, even after the end of the working day, are engrossed in their intricate designs and who are pursued, into their dreams, by the feeling that they have got hold of the wrong thread. On the other hand, when we consider the weavers' mental illnesses we should also bear in mind that many of the materials produced in the factories of Norwich in the decades before the Industrial Revolution began – silk brocades and watered tabinets, satins and satinettes, camblets and cheveretts, prunelles, callimancoes and florentines, diamantines and grenadines, blondines, bombazines, belle-isles and martiniques – were of a truly fabulous variety, and of an iridescent, quite indescribable beauty as if they had been produced by Nature itself, like the plumage of birds. – That, at any rate, is what I think when I look at the marvellous strips of colour in the pattern books, the edges and gaps filled with mysterious figures and symbols, that are kept in the small museum of Strangers Hall, which was once the town house of just such a family of silk weavers who had been exiled from France.

	68	bro: up	
236	2 4		Spencer 2 Crop Swithin 2
237	4		Knight Dan 2 Smith Sam 2
238	4		Knight Nat 2 Barry Thos 2
239	3 4		Edgegood Rd 2 Johnson Wm 2
240	4		Waller Robt 2 Carver Jn 2
241	2		Doughty Wm 2
243	2		Duffield Jas
244	2		Love Thos
245	2		Jenkinson
246	3 4		Harvey Jos 2 Smoulton Wm 2
247	1 4		Snelling Wm 2 Duffield Jas 2
248	2		Knights Dan
249	2		Brown Chas
250	2		Hutcher Ben

Lappits hanging out.

110 S Camblets 21 .. 30

20.4d

Lemon & Green Edges with a Scarlet End

L

This Supplement of Camblets to go to Cooke.

2.5.3
38
1212
13.7

29 June 1797

1	2		Smith Sam

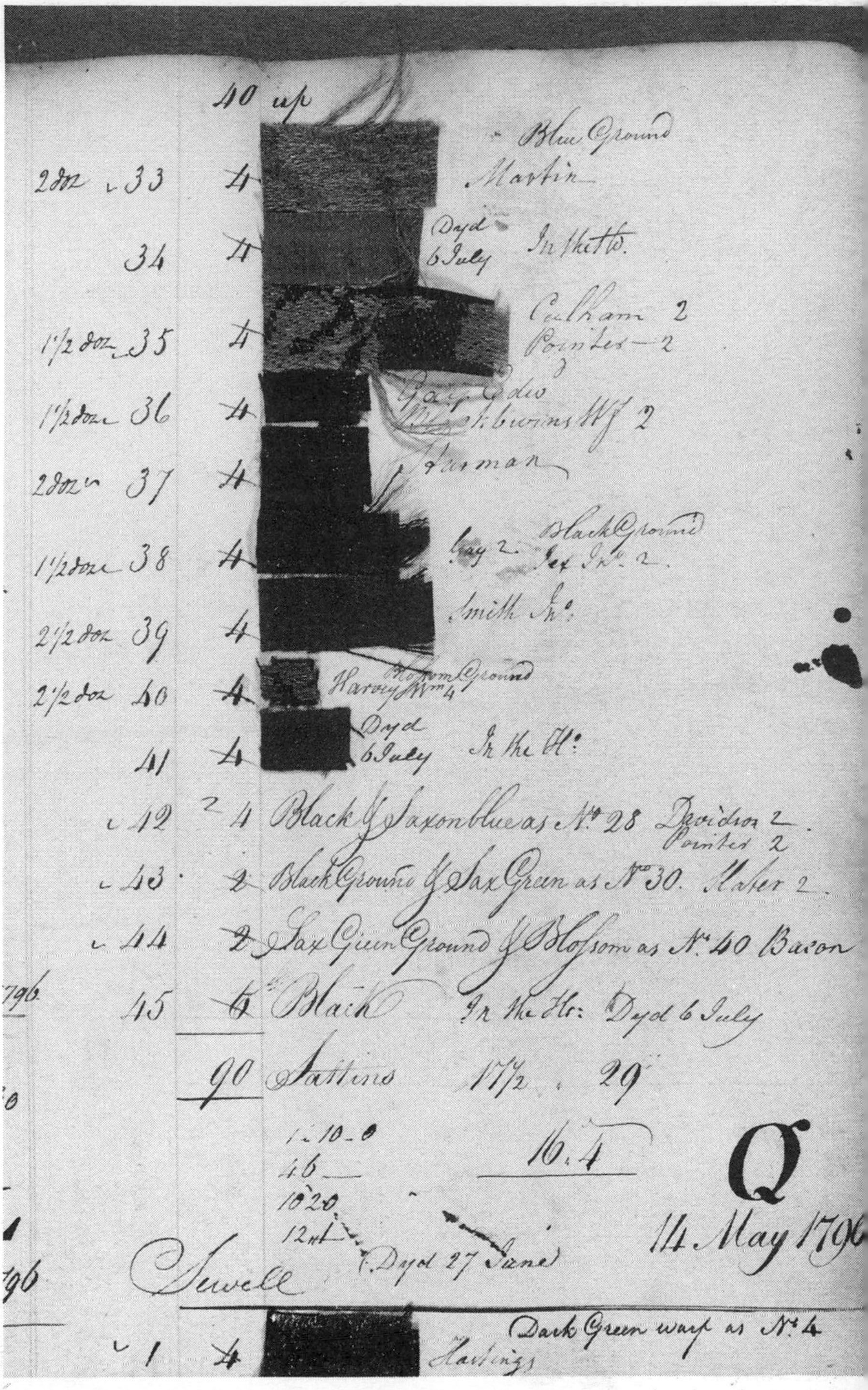
40 up

Blue Ground

2doz 33 4 Martin

34 4 Dyd 6 July In the Ho.

1½ doz 35 4 Culham 2

Pointer 2

1½ doz 36 4 Gay do

Browns Wf 2

2doz 37 4 Harman

Black Ground

1½ doz 38 4 Gay 2 Ice Jno. 2

2½ doz 39 4 Smith Jno.

Blossom Ground

2½ doz 40 4 Harvey Wm 4

41 4 Dyd 6 July In the Ho.

42 2 4 Black & Saxonblue as No. 28 Davidson 2

Pointer 2

43 2 Black Ground & Sax Green as No 30. Maker 2.

44 2 Sax Green Ground & Blossom as No. 40 Bacon

1796 45 6 Black In the Ho: Dyd 6 July

90 Sattins 17/2 . 29

1.10.0

46

10 20

12st

16.4

Q

Dyd 27 June

14 May 1796

Sewell

1 4 Dark Green warp as No. 4

Hastings

Until the decline of the Norwich manufactories towards the end of the eighteenth century, these catalogues of samples, the pages of which seem to me to be leaves from the only true book which none of our textual and pictorial works can even begin to rival, were to be found in the offices of importers throughout Europe, from Riga to Rotterdam and from St Petersburg to Seville. And the materials themselves were sent from Norwich to the trade fairs at Copenhagen, Leipzig and Zurich, and from there to the warehouses of wholesalers and retailers, and some half-silk wedding shawl might even reach Isny, Weingarten or Wangen in the pannier on a Jewish pedlar's back.

The greatest efforts were made to promote the cultivation of silk, even in the rather backward Germany of the time, where pigs were still being driven across the Schlossplatz in many a principal town. In Prussia, Frederick the Great with the help of French immigrants had attempted to bring a state silk industry into being, by ordering mulberry plantations to be established, by distributing silkworms free of charge, and by offering considerable rewards to anyone who would take up silk cultivation. In 1774, about seven thousand pounds of pure silk were produced in the provinces of Magdeburg, Halberstadt, Brandenburg and Pomerania alone. The same happened in Saxony, the county of Hanau, in Württemberg, Ansbach and Bayreuth, on the Prince of Liechtenstein's estates in Austria, and in the Rhineland-Palatinate at the bidding of Karl Theodor who, when the succession of the duchy of Bavaria passed to him in 1777, at once set up a silk head office in Munich. Forthwith, extensive mulberry gardens were established in Freising, Egelkofen, Landshut, Burghausen, Straubing and in the state capital itself. The trees were planted along paths, ramparts and roads, silk houses and filatories were built, factories were set up and a host of officials employed. Despite being promoted with such vigour in Bavaria and other German principalities, silk manufacturing ground to a halt even before it had properly begun. The mulberry gardens disappeared, the trees were felled for firewood, the officials were pensioned off, and the steaming vats, filature machines and rearing frames were broken up, sold or carried off. On the 1st of April 1822, the Director of the Royal Gardens informed the General Committee of the Agricultural Association that an old master dyer by the name of Seybolt, who, according to a file still in the Munich state library was employed for nine years at a salary of three hundred and fifty florins in the silk factory run by the previous government as Keeper of the Silkworms and Superintendent of Carding and Filature, had told the said director that in his time many thousands of mulberry trees had been planted and numbered, on orders from on high, throughout the city, and that these trees had grown to an astounding size affording much excellent provender for the grubs. Of those trees, Seybolt said, only two remained, one in the garden of von Utzschneider's textile factory by the Einlass Gate, and the other, as far as he knew, in the garden of the former Augustinian monastery, where the monks had made some modest attempts at silk farming. The main reason why silk husbandry failed so soon after it had been introduced was not so much that the mercantile calculations were adrift, but rather the despotic manner in which German rulers attempted to force it along, whatever the cost. From a memorandum from Count von Reigersberg, the Bavarian ambassador to Karlsruhe, referring to reports submitted by a certain Herr Kall, who was the only plantation inspector still employed in sericulture at Schwetzingen, it emerges that in the Rhineland-Palatinate, where silk farming had been conducted on the largest scale, every subject, official, citizen and householder who owned more than an acre of land was obliged within a given period to be growing six trees per acre, regardless of his circumstances or the use to which he had hitherto devoted his fields. Whosoever had been granted arms-bearing, brewing or baking rights had to plant one tree, every newly accredited citizen had to plant two, all village greens, town squares, streets, embankments, boundary ditches, even churchyards had to be planted, so that subjects were compelled to buy a hundred thousand trees from the principality's tree nurseries every year. Planting and tending the mulberry trees was imposed as a personal duty on the twelve youngest citizens in every community. In addition, there were the costs involved in employing twenty-nine officials responsible for silk cultivation, as well as special supervisors in each individual town or village, who were exempted from socage service, granted certain liberties, and paid forty-five crowns a day. Part of the costs which arose from this decree had to be met from communal funds, and part was levied through taxation. Such a burden, which was by no means justified by the true economic value of the silk industry, together with the extreme financial and physical penalties for transgressing against the silk laws, succeeded in making something that had been viewed as a promising venture hateful to the people; it led to endless petitions, applications for concessions, litigation and court cases, which for years overwhelmed the higher judicial and administrative authorities with paperwork until, upon the death of Karl Theodor, the Elector Max Joseph cut the ground from under this rampant absurdity by revoking all the compulsory measures once and for all.

The reports made to the Imperial Royal Counsellor of War in Vienna in 1811, at about the same time as silk cultivation in Germany collapsed, by the border regiments to whom research into outdoor silk cultivation had been entrusted, were also anything but encouraging. Memoranda that were almost identical in content arrived, drawn up by Colonels Michalevics and Hordinsky of the Wallachian-Illyrian regiment in Caransebes and the 12th German Banat regiment in Pancsova, to the effect that, after initial hopes of being able to nurture the broods in their care, they had been adversely affected by storms and cloudbursts, and in some cases, in Glogau, Perlasvarosch and Isbitie, where they had sloughed their skins for the first time, and in Homolitz and Oppowa, where they had done so a second time, they had been knocked off the foliage by hailstones and perished. Moreover, the memoranda continued, the caterpillars were at the mercy of numerous enemies, such as sparrows and starlings, which devoured them as soon as they were set in the trees. Colonel Minitinovich of the Gradiskan regiment complained of the worms' lack of appetite, of the changeable weather, of gnats, wasps and flies, while Colonel Milletich of the 7th Brod border regiment reported that, by the 12th of July, the few silkworms and evolving papillons that had survived on the trees had been burned by the fierce heat of that summer, or else, unable to graze on the now tough and leathery leaves, had simply expired. Despite these setbacks, Bavarian Counsellor of State Joseph von Hazzi undertook to advocate sericulture in his *Lehrbuch des Seidenbaus für Deutschland* of 1826, avoiding, wherever possible, the errors that had been made in the past and emphasizing instead its importance in the formation of a national economy. Hazzi's work, which was conceived as a complete educational programme, followed on from that published in Milan in 1810 by Count Dandolo, *Dell arte di governare i bachi da Setta*, from Bonafou's *De l'éducation des vers à soie*, Bolzano's *Wegweiser zum Seidenbau* and Kettenbeil's *Anleitung zur Behandlung des Maulbeerbaums und Erziehung der Seidenraupe.* If the German silk industry were to be revived, wrote Hazzi, it was essential to recognize the mistakes that had been made, which in his opinion had resulted from authoritarian management, endeavours to create state monopolies, and an administrative system which buried any entrepreneurial spirit under a quite risible pile of regulations. In Hazzi's view, silk cultivation did not require special buildings and institutes, which would always be costly and would look like barracks or hospitals, but instead, as was the case in Greece and Italy, it should be born out of nothing, as it were, and be run as a minor pursuit in domestic rooms and chambers by women and children, servants, the poor and the elderly, in short, by all who were not at present in a position to earn money. Placing silk cultivation on a popular footing in the way Hazzi recommended would not only lead to incontestable economic advantages over other nations, it would also result in the social improvement of the fair sex and all other members of the populace who were unaccustomed to regular work. In addition, observing this apparently insignificant insect, and how it develops in stages under man's care and brings forth the softest and most delicate of tissues, would provide an invaluable and fitting aid for the education of children. In Hazzi's estimation, there could be no more convenient way of inculcating among the lower classes the virtues of order and cleanliness, which were indispensable to all communities, than the widespread cultivation of silk; indeed he would expect, wrote Hazzi, that the breeding of silkworms in the homes of most German families would produce a veritable moral transformation in the nation. Hazzi then goes on to deal with various misconceptions and prejudices connected with silk cultivation, such as that the best place to hatch silkworms was in hotbeds or the bosoms of young girls, or that, once they had hatched, one should heat up the stove on cool days, close the shutters during thunderstorms, and hang bunches of wormwood in windows to dispel harmful miasmas. It would be far more sensible, according to Hazzi, to air the rooms daily and, if necessary, fumigate them at little expense with chlorine gas produced by mixing sea salt, powdered manganese and a little water. Jaundice, consumption and other diseases to which the worms were susceptible could thus be easily avoided, and a cottage industry altogether useful and profitable would be as good as assured by the proliferation of this new knowledge through ever widening circles. Counsellor Hazzi's vision of a nation united by sericulture and educating itself toward higher ends went unheeded, doubtless because the previous failures lay in the too recent past. However, after an interval of a hundred years it was revived by the German fascists with that peculiar thoroughness they brought to everything they touched, as I realized with some surprise when, last summer, searching in the education office of the town I grew up in for the short documentary about North Sea herring fisheries which had been shown to us in primary school, I happened upon a film on German silk cultivation, evidently made for the same series. In contrast to the dark, almost midnight tonalities of the herring film, the film on sericulture was of a truly dazzling brightness. Men and women in white coats, in whitewashed rooms flooded with light, were busy at snow-white spinning frames, snow-white sheets of paper, snow-white protective gauze, snow-white cocoons and snow-white canvas mailing sacks. The whole film promised the best and cleanest of all possible worlds, an impression that was confirmed when I read the accompanying booklet, which was intended for our teachers. Citing

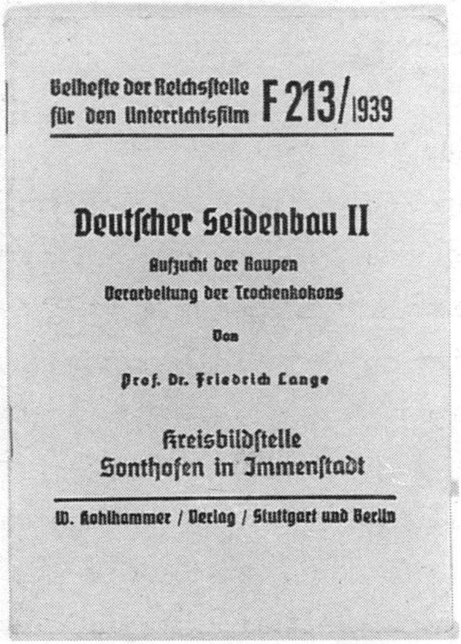
Beihefte der Reichsstelle für den Unterrichtsfilm F 213/1939

Deutscher Seidenbau II

Aufzucht der Raupen
Verarbeitung der Trockenkokons

Von

Prof. Dr. Friedrich Lange

Kreisbildstelle
Sonthofen in Immenstadt

W. Kohlhammer / Verlag / Stuttgart und Berlin

the Führer's pronouncement, at the 1936 party rally, that Germany must become self-sufficient within four years in all the materials it lay in the nation's power to produce itself, the author of the booklet observed that this self-evidently included silk cultivation.

Hence the Reich ministers of food and agriculture, of labour, of forestry and of aviation had launched a sericulture programme, inaugurating a new era of silk cultivation in Germany. The Reich Association of Silkworm Breeders in Berlin, a constitutent group within the Reich Federation of German Breeders of Small Animals, which in turn was affiliated to the Reich Agricultural Commission, saw its task as increasing production in every existing workshop, advertising silk cultivation in the press, in the cinema and on radio, establishing model rearing units for educational purposes, organizing advisory bodies at local, district and regional level to support all silk-growers, providing mulberry trees, and planting them by the million on unutilized land, in residential areas and cemeteries, by roadsides, on railway embankments and along the Reich's autobahns. According to Professor Lange, the author of educational pamphlet F213/1939, the significance of silk cultivation in Germany lay not only in obviating the need to buy from abroad, and so easing the pressure on foreign currency reserves, but also in the importance silk would have in the dawning era of aerial warfare and hence in the formation of a self-sufficient economy of national defence. For that reason, it was desirable that schools should interest the youth of Germany in silk cultivation, although not under compulsion, as in the days of Frederick the Great. Rather, the teaching staff and pupils should be motivated to practise sericulture of their own accord. Schools might do pioneering work in this sector, suggested Professor Lange. Schoolyards might have mulberries planted along their perimeters, and silkworms could be reared in the school buildings. After all, the Professor added, quite apart from their indubitable utility value, silkworms afforded an almost ideal object lesson for the classroom. Any number could be had for virtually nothing, they were perfectly docile and needed neither cages nor compounds, and they were suitable for a variety of experiments (weighing, measuring and so forth) at every stage in their evolution. They could be used to illustrate the structure and distinctive features of insect anatomy, insect domestication, retrogressive mutations, and the essential measures which are taken by breeders to monitor productivity and selection, including extermination to preempt racial degeneration. – In the film, we see a silk-worker receiving eggs despatched by the Central Reich Institute of Sericulture in Celle, and depositing them in sterile trays. We see the hatching, the feeding of the ravenous caterpillars, the cleaning out of the frames, the spinning of the silken thread, and finally the killing, accomplished in this case not by putting the cocoons out in the sun or in a hot oven, as was often the practice in the past, but by suspending them over a boiling cauldron. The cocoons, spread out on shallow baskets, have to be kept in the rising steam for upwards of three hours, and when a batch is done, it is the next one's turn, and so on until the entire killing business is completed.

Today, as I bring these notes to a conclusion, is the 13th of April 1995. It is Maundy Thursday, the feast day on which Christ's washing of the disciples' feet is remembered, and also the feast day of Saints Agathon, Carpus, Papylus and Hermengild. On this very day three hundred and ninety-seven years ago, Henry IV promulgated the Edict of Nantes; Handel's *Messiah* was first performed two hundred and fifty-three years ago, in Dublin; Warren Hastings was appointed Governor-General of Bengal two hundred and twenty-three years ago; the Anti-Semitic League was founded in Prussia one hundred and thirteen years ago; and, seventy-four years ago, the Amritsar massacre occurred, when General Dyer ordered his troops to fire on a rebellious crowd of fifteen thousand that had gathered in Jallianwala Bagh square, to set an example. Quite possibly some of the victims were employed in silk cultivation, which was developing at that time, on the simplest of foundations, in the Amritsar region and indeed throughout India.

Fifty years ago to the day, British newspapers reported that the city of Celle had been taken and that German forces were in headlong retreat from the Red Army, which was advancing up the Danube valley. And finally, Maundy Thursday, the 13th of April 1995, was also the day on which Clara's father, shortly after being taken to hospital in Coburg, departed this life. Now, as I write, and think once more of our history, which is but a long account of calamities, it occurs to me that at one time the only acceptable expression of profound grief, for ladies of the upper classes, was to wear heavy robes of black silk taffeta or black crêpe de chine. Thus at Queen Victoria's funeral, for example, the Duchess of Teck allegedly made her appearance in what contemporary fashion magazines described as a breathtaking gown with billowing veils, all of black Mantua silk of which the Norwich silk weavers Willett & Nephew, just before the firm closed down for good, had created, uniquely for this occasion, and in order to demonstrate their unsurpassed skills in the manufacture of mourning silks, a length of some sixty paces. And Sir Thomas Browne, who was the son of a silk merchant and may well have had an eye for these things, remarks in a passage of the *Pseudodoxia Epidemica* that I can no longer find that in the Holland of his time it was customary, in a home where there had been a death, to drape black mourning ribbons over all the mirrors and all canvasses depicting landscapes or people or the fruits of the field, so that the soul, as it left the body, would not be distracted on its final journey, either by a reflection of itself or by a last glimpse of the land now being lost for ever.